VISIONS *of*
AFRICA

To everybody who travels through Africa, its parks and reserves – it is your contribution
that benefits Africa and its people, and preserves its wildlife for future generations.

VISIONS of AFRICA

DAVID WALL

NEW HOLLAND

First published in 1998 by
New Holland (Publishers) Ltd
London • Cape Town • Sydney • Singapore

24 Nutford Place	80 McKenzie Street	3/2 Aquatic Drive
London W1H 6DQ	Cape Town 8001	Frenchs Forest,
United Kingdom	South Africa	NSW 2086, Australia

ISBN 1 85368 966 1

10 9 8 7 6 5 4 3 2

Managing editor: Annlerie van Rooyen
Editor: Glynne Newlands
Designer: Laurence Lemmon-Warde
Design Assistants: Lellyn Creamer and Sonia Hedenskog
Cartographer: Desireé Oosterberg
Indexer: Lesley Hay-Whitton
Reproduction by Hirt & Carter Cape (Pty) Ltd
Printed and bound in Singapore by Tien Wah Press (Pte) Ltd

FRONT COVER *Dawn on the Congo River.*
BACK COVER *Sossusvlei in the Namib Desert, Namibia.*
SPINE *Lioness, Masai Mara National Reserve, Kenya.*
ENDPAPERS *Silk carpet, Morocco.*
HALF TITLE PAGE *Kokerboom, or quiver tree, in Namibia.*
TITLE PAGES *Dunes in the Namib Desert, Namibia.*
THIS PAGE *Elephants at sunset, Amboseli National Park, Kenya.*
FOLLOWING PAGES *Sunrise over Dar es Salaam harbour, Tanzania.*

ACKNOWLEDGEMENTS
If it were not for the continual support of Jude, my wife, this book would still be a
bulldog clip full of hand-written notes, and plastic boxes full of slides. Thanks to Kerry
Butler, who introduced both Jude and myself to Africa a decade ago. The chance to
work for Kerry and 'Wifey' taking overland expeditions across Africa led to the
collection of photographs and gave us first-hand experience of over 25 countries. To
Andy Kibby, Mark Kroon and the 'family' of overland crews, thanks for the camaraderie
and cold primus. I would especially like to thank my sister Judith for putting up with
my persistent use of her computer until I finally got my own. I am very grateful to
Struik, my publishers, for their faith in my proposal, and particularly to my editor,
Glynne, and to Annlerie, for all their work and support. Thanks also to Laurence, the
designer, and Dez for the maps, and to everyone at Struik who worked on this project.

PHOTOGRAPHIC CREDITS
ABPL = Anthony Bannister Photo Library; **MVA-PE** = Mark van Aardt - Photographic Enterprises;
PA = Photo Access; **SIL** = Struik Image Library
Imprint page: **A Bannister/SIL**; Contents page: **P Ribton/SIL**; p. 9: **CLI/PA**; p. 10: **MVA-PE**;
p. 30: **L von Hörsten/SIL**; p. 34: **H Potgieter**; pp. 46-47: **PA**; p. 49: **D Rogers** (PA-Getaway);
p. 51: **P Wagner** (PA-Getaway); p. 52: **D Rogers** (PA-Getaway); p. 58: **D Rogers** (PA-Getaway);
p. 59: **P Wagner** (PA-Getaway); p. 62: **PA**; p. 63: **D Rogers** (PA-Getaway); pp. 64-65:
W Griffiths/ABPL; p. 66: **G Spiby**; p. 67: **D Kohler**; pp. 68-69: **D Rogers** (PA-Getaway); p. 82:
V Englebert; p. 112: **D Balfour/SIL**; p. 115: **P Ribton/SIL**; p. 117: **P de la Harpe**; pp. 120-121:
A Bannister/SIL; p. 126: **P Blackwell/SIL**; p. 127: **D Balfour/SIL**; pp. 128-129: **D Balfour/SIL**;
p. 130: **P Blackwell/SIL**; pp. 132-133: **R de la Harpe/SIL**; p. 137: **K Begg/SIL**; p. 138:
K Begg/SIL; p. 141: **D Balfour**; pp. 144-145: **W Knirr/SIL**; p. 147: **N Dennis/SIL**; p. 148:
W Knirr/SIL; pp. 149-150: **R de la Harpe/SIL**; p. 153: **D Balfour**; pp. 154-155: **D Balfour**;
p. 156: **P Pickford/SIL**; pp. 158-159: **D Balfour**; pp. 160-161: **G Dreyer/SIL**; p. 162: **W Knirr**;
p. 163: **M Lewis/SIL**; pp. 164-165: **H von Hörsten/SIL**

CONTENTS

INTRODUCTION

kingdoms dripping in gold, and diamonds so abundant in the Namib Desert that they sparkled in the moonlight. Like the early explorers' reports of 'man-beasts' (gorillas) in the jungle and snow and ice on the equator, these myths and legends were thought to be just that. But as we now know, they were all true.

The vast continent of Africa cannot be stereotyped. Some think of it as a hot, dry continent but it has 49 glaciers within a degree of the equator. Ethiopia, often depicted as a dusty, barren desert, has a large mountainous region that provides the majority of the water for the river Nile. In Botswana is the Okavango, the world's largest inland delta – a wetland with luxuriant vegetation and abundant wildlife – surrounded by the arid Kalahari Desert.

More than any other continent, Africa is known for its wildlife. Here the 'Big Five' (lion, leopard, rhinoceros, elephant and buffalo) can be seen, and other animals of every shape, size and colour, living in a variety of habitats – from gorillas and chimps of the rainforest to desert-dwelling gemsbok and springbok. But it is in-between these two extremes where African wildlife is at its most prolific. On the savannas and plains of East and Southern Africa, a daily spectacle unfolds that no other continent can match for diversity and numbers.

It is not only wildlife safaris, however, that draw people to Africa but also its many magnificent sights. It boasts the only fully surviving Wonder of the Ancient World, the Great Pyramids in Egypt, and Zimbabwe and Zambia's breathtaking Victoria Falls, a Natural Wonder of the World. There are less well-known

Very few books on Africa begin without using the word 'diverse' – whether describing the continent as a whole, its scenery, its people and cultures, or its wildlife. The 55 nations of Africa embrace landscapes from desert to tropical rainforest to icecap, and within individual countries are ethnic groups that number in the hundreds, each with their own language or dialect: there are over 50 different languages that each have more than a million speakers.

The name Africa evokes different images to different people. To some it may be the fictional jungles of Tarzan, while to others it is the vast, uninhabited deserts, or the open plains of the savanna teeming with wildlife. Many will think of Africa's great mysteries – searching for the Mountains of the Moon, the Great Lakes, the sources of the Nile, Zambezi and Congo rivers, or King Solomon's mines. Myths and legends abound, such as the desert city of Timbuktu, the hidden treasures of the pharaohs, West African

ABOVE *A magnificent male lion in Kenya's Masai Mara National Reserve.*
OPPOSITE *The 3 300-year-old gold mask of the Egyptian Pharaoh, Tutankhamen.*

natural phenomena, such as the Namib Desert's giant dunescapes in Namibia, and volcanic plugs forming massive rock pinnacles at Roumsiki in Cameroon. In Tanzania tens of thousands of mammals are surrounded by the 600-metre-high (1 970 feet) walls of Ngorongoro Crater, a massive collapsed volcano. At the tip of the continent lies South Africa's flat-topped Table Mountain on the Cape Peninsula, described by Sir Francis Drake as '... the fairest cape in the whole circumference of the earth'.

On this continent, sizes are not always easy to comprehend. The Nile River, for example, is an incredible 6 670 kilometres (4 144 miles) long. Lake Victoria is half the size of England while the catchment area for the Congo River is roughly the size of Western Europe. The Congo River itself is nearly 5 000 kilometres (3 106 miles) long – the same as the width of the world's largest desert, the Sahara.

While Africa's dimensions are impressive, it hides secrets that are just as fascinating. In the West and North are windows to a time that existed centuries ago. Pockets of age-old tradition are to be found throughout West Africa, with large camel caravans occasionally trekking across the Sahara even today. Parts of ancient trading cities like Kano and Timbuktu in the south, and Fez and Marrakech in the north, operate as they did in mediaeval times. Sultanates and kingdoms still function across West Africa, and in North Africa, particularly along the Mediterranean coast and the Nile River, are some of the world's most complete ancient ruins, from several civilizations.

But there is more to Africa than its ancient history, prolific wildlife, superb panoramas and varied cultures – it has something intangible that affects not only those who live there but also visitors who experience solitude in its wilderness, excitement in its game parks, awe in its landscapes and vibrancy in its people.

HISTORY

The story of mankind begins in Africa. Scientists believe that somewhere in our distant past, several million years ago, all races of the world are linked to a common African ancestor. But the chain of evolution goes back further than this, to creatures more like apes than humans but who are still classified as hominids by their bipedal, or upright, walking stance.

Most of the significant early man sites are along East Africa's Great Rift Valley. One of the first places to become prominent was Olduvai Gorge between Tanzania's Serengeti National Park and Ngorongoro Crater. It was here in 1959, after more than two decades of work by Mary and Louis Leakey, that Mary finally made an extremely important discovery – a skull and jaws 1.8 million years old. Twenty years later a short distance away at Laetoli, Mary Leakey found something else that pushed back bipedalism even further. This time it was the footprints of two hominids, who three million

six hundred thousand years ago walked across an ash-covered plain in the shadow of an active volcano. The ash from Sadiman, a volcano near the edge of Ngorongoro Crater, combined with just the right amount of light rain to cement the footprints into history.

In 1974, further up the Great Rift Valley at Hadar, Ethiopia, paleoanthropologist Donald Johanson found a 40 percent complete fossil skeleton that was dated at 3.18 million years old. Now regarded as one of the most noteworthy finds, the skeleton was named Lucy after a popular Beatles song. In 1975, fossils from another 13 individuals were unearthed nearby by Johanson's team.

In the south of Ethiopia, in the remote Omo Valley, hominid remains over two million years old have been identified, while just across the border in Kenya, Lake Turkana has also revealed several fossil sites. New discoveries over two million years old have recently been found in Malawi, and sites in South Africa have turned up hundreds of hominid fossils between two and three million years old.

Over the ages, hominids developed from using stone tools to fire. Today two groups of people in Africa give insight into the early lifestyle of people who lived off the land without keeping livestock or using agriculture: the hunter-gatherers. The San (Bushmen) of the dry southern regions and the Pygmies of the African rainforests both have a respect for and unique knowledge of their environment. In this aspect they are light years ahead of modern societies, being of the few peoples who can live without destroying their surroundings.

The hunter-gatherer lifestyle sustained mankind for around four million years, until about 10 000 years ago when agriculture was introduced – in other words, for 99.75 percent of the time that man has walked the planet, he has been a hunter-gatherer.

VISIONS OF AFRICA

NORTH AFRICAN CIVILIZATIONS

Ancient Egypt was one of the world's first great civilizations, comparable at the time only to Mesopotamia, situated in what is modern-day Iraq. From these two early cultures came inventions such as writing, the wheel and boats – developments that European civilizations would later borrow from Africa and the Middle East to advance their own progress. Other remarkable efforts of the Egyptians are the Great Pyramids of Giza which, when built around 2500BC, were the largest stone structures in the world. Even today, four and a half millennia later, few edifices can compare to them.

In the 8th century BC the Egyptians were conquered by another African kingdom – the Kushites from what is now Sudan. The Kingdom of Kush is said to have supplied Egypt with much of its gold, possibly tens of thousands of kilograms per year. Like the Egyptian pharaohs, the Kushite kings built

pyramids and underground burial chambers filled with treasure, and as in Egypt, the treasure from most of the tombs was plundered long ago. Kushite ruins, including many pyramids, can be seen at several sites along the Nile River in Sudan. The Kushites only held onto Egypt for about 60 years before the Assyrians pushed them back south, where they were later conquered by the Ethiopians.

The short Assyrian reign was part of a period during which Egypt was ruled by foreigners. Among them were Nebuchadnezzar of Babylon (who built the Hanging Gardens) and later the Persians, but it was the Greeks, under Alexander the Great, who took Egypt in 332BC and held it for 300 years. The young 25-year-old Alexander ordered a new capital to be built – Alexandria – but this was not the first Greek city to be developed along the North African coastline: Cyrene in Libya was founded by the Greeks around 630BC. For centuries the Greeks and Phoenicians, the two main

seafaring nations at the time, had built cities along the Mediterranean coast, particularly in what is now Libya and Tunisia. They vied for control with the indigenous Berbers, who had a stronghold on the trans-Saharan trade. The Berbers were known for their four-horse charioteering (which the Greeks later learnt from them), and also had an elephant cavalry. Not until the first century AD did the camel with its natural advantages in the desert come to dominate trans-Saharan trade.

The Romans replaced the Greeks and Phoenicians as trading partners, and North Africa became Rome's bread-basket. Under Julius Caesar the Roman Republic developed into an empire, expanding its dominance right across North Africa. Just before Caesar's death in 44BC, a new calendar originated from Egypt, with the month of July named after Julius, and August and October after his adopted son Octavian, also known as Augustus.

Five centuries later Islam swept across North Africa. Within a century of Prophet Mohammed's death in 632AD, Muslim Arabs had not only taken all of North Africa, but they crossed to Europe, pushing through Spain and Portugal as far as southern France. Islam spread westward across Africa north of the Sahara Desert, as well as west across the Sahel and south along the East African coast. In West Africa, where strong traditional religions held sway, Islam was slower to take root. But it did enhance empires like Mali and Songhay with

LEFT *Lost to the world for centuries until found by a Swiss traveller in 1813 is the Small Temple at Abu Simble in Egypt.*
OPPOSITE *Dating back to the 13th and 14th centuries, and with walls several metres thick, is the narrow parallel passage in Southern Africa's medieval city of Great Zimbabwe.*

its advantages of education, writing and trade with the rest of the Muslim world. It was in the west that a series of important kingdoms emerged in the middle of the first millennium.

WEST AFRICAN KINGDOMS

The oral folklore and songs of West Africa recall stories of battles of the distant past, of great kingdoms, and of kings who were adorned with gold and attended by hundreds of slaves. Many of the tales concur with the written accounts of ancient travellers from the north who describe the successive great West African empires of Ghana, Mali and Songhay.

Around 500AD the empire of Ghana (connected in name only to modern-day Ghana) sprung up in West Africa and grew to control much of the trans-Saharan trade. Ghana (meaning 'king') had its capital at Koumbi-Saleh, now in the south-east corner of Mauritania. Its kingdom ranged along the Sahel from around the Niger River bend near Timbuktu, as far west as Senegal. Like later West African empires, it became known for its vast riches of gold. Despite accounts of a 200 000-strong army, Ghana inevitably attracted invaders and eventually Berber Muslims took the empire in 1076.

Under their control, the empire went into decline and collapsed into smaller states, with one of these, Kangaba, growing in power. The Mandinka people of Kangaba on the upper Niger River conquered neighbouring states and by 1240 had become a major power in the region. Their state became the Mali Empire which eventually grew to dominate a large area from the western tip of Africa, eastward for about 2 000 kilometres (1 243 miles) to the northern boundaries of modern Nigeria. It also controlled and taxed trade between the rich southern goldfields and states north of the Sahara – North Africa, Europe and Asia. A

surprising range of commodities were traded, from Egyptian thoroughbred horses to wool, leather, dried fruit and olive oil from North Africa. From Europe and Asia came perfumes, spices, silks, timber, textiles and glass, and from West Africa came copper and salt from the Sahara as well as gold in vast quantities. While gold was the main currency, cowrie shells from the Maldives in the Indian Ocean were used as small change.

However, it was because of gold that the Empire of Mali became famous. The empire's most notable leader was Mansa Musa, who as a Muslim made a Hajj to Mecca (Saudi Arabia), taking with him an entourage estimated at 8 000 to 15 000 people. He distributed so much gold as gifts to the people of Cairo that he depressed the gold market for many years.

Not long after Mansa Musa's death in 1337, the great world traveller Ibn Battuta crossed the Sahara to Mali. Although remarking that the

people of Mali were very miserly towards him, he was impressed with the ease of travel, good security and honesty in the region, and the people's sense of justice and rule of the law.

But by 1375 there was much in-fighting in Mali and the Songhay declared independence with their capital in Gão on the Niger River. The Songhay empire soon took over from Mali to control an area almost as great in size, but further to the east. Gold, ivory and slaves were in such abundance that they influenced the economies of those European countries who relied on African gold for their currencies. The Songhay empire grew in power with a navy of 400 war canoes, but came to an abrupt end when it was invaded by Berbers from Morocco in 1591. By this time Europeans had started setting up trading bases along the west coast and trade routes began focusing south towards sea ports instead of north across the Sahara.

At the same time as the empires of Ghana, Mali and Songhay flourished, a fourth and separate empire controlled an area to the east. Around 800AD the Kanem-Bornu Empire gained momentum in the region around Lake Chad, and although it never had control of the gold trade in the way the empires further west did, it did rise to substantial greatness with diplomatic missions in Tripoli and Cairo by 1571. A thousand years after the empire's beginning, British explorers dismissed legends of its cavalry of black knights in chain mail suits, only to be confronted by them in 1823. The explorers were welcomed with a series of mock charges by the cavalry.

From around 1000AD smaller city states in what is now northern Nigeria gained power in trans-Saharan trade, and other kingdoms grew up nearer the coast. The most prominent of these was the Kingdom of Benin, a powerful state in what is today's southern Nigeria (but not within the country that now calls itself

Benin). By about the mid-15th century it was trading peacefully with the Portuguese. European travellers to Benin were astonished at what they found: a 10-kilometre-long (6 mile) wall with a five-storey-deep moat surrounded the inner city of approximately 60 000 people. The Oba, or King, had a palace with 100 courtyards. Wooden columns holding up the ceilings were covered in brass plaques that depicted significant events and honoured warriors, Obas and hunters. Between 6 000 and 12 000 kilometres (3 728 and 7 456 miles) of earthen walls marked its boundaries in the rural areas, and are considered to be the world's largest earthworks of pre-mechanical times.

While northern states and empires were strongly influenced by Islam, which helped structure their civilizations with the advantage of written language, the Kingdom of Benin was animist, often practising human sacrifice. Fearing reprisal from the British after a consul was ambushed and killed by a rogue chief, the Oba sought protection from the spirits through sacrifice. The British arrived at Benin City in 1897 to a gruesome sight: a mass slaughter of hundreds of people. They also found the bronze statues and plaques for which Benin is now famous – 2 000 pieces were taken to Europe to be auctioned off as spoils of war.

Kanem-Bornu, Songhay, Mali, Ghana and the Kingdom of Benin were not the only great African kingdoms south of the Sahara. While the animist and Islamic empires of the west waxed and waned, across the continent a much older African empire outlived them all.

EAST AND SOUTHERN AFRICAN KINGDOMS
As Islam spread across Africa it left a conspicuous island of Christianity in the Ethiopian Highlands. Virtually all Christianity has been brought to Africa in the last century

or two, but Ethiopia has had its own form of Christianity since the 4th century AD. Ethiopia, literally meaning 'burnt faces', was originally the name given to all of the unknown regions south of Egypt. The Ethiopians, previously called Abyssinians, can trace their emperors back to around 1000BC, in a line of dynasties that span three millennia. Ethiopian civilization kept much to itself but boasted incredible achievements, such as the erection of large stone stelae at Ethiopia's first capital, Axum. Hundreds of monolithic churches are also found in the Ethiopian Highlands – churches not built but carved from stone. Many of these churches are in locations so remote that they are virtually unknown to the outside world.

BELOW *This priest, like millions of other Ethiopians, adheres to an ancient indigenous form of Christianity over 1 000 years old.* OPPOSITE *St Georges Church in Lalibela, Ethiopia, carved from a single piece of stone.*

The Ethiopians came to rule over the Kushites of Sudan, who had previously ruled Egypt, as well as over parts of the Middle East across the Red Sea. At their height in the 6th century AD, the Ethiopians were a major world power, trading with both Asia and Europe. With the advantage of their own written language and calendar, the Ethiopian Kingdom was arguably one of the more advanced and long-lived kingdoms of the African interior.

But the Arabs and their ocean-going dhows, and Islam, had for centuries influenced the East African coast. Because of the need for Arab slavers and traders to communicate with local Africans, the Swahili language and culture was born. Arab influence reached a peak on the East African island of Zanzibar when, after being ruled from Muscat in the Middle East, the Omani Arabs moved their capital to Zanzibar in 1832.

By the time Portuguese sailor Vasco da Gama had 'discovered' East Africa in 1498, the region had already been trading across the oceans for at least 13 centuries. Trade routes reached as far afield as India, the Indonesian islands near Australia, and China. The trade with China along Africa's Indian Ocean helps explain the existence of fragments of early Chinese porcelain that were found inland at the site of a significant Southern African civilization: Great Zimbabwe.

Great Zimbabwe, in the country that has now taken its name from it, had its beginnings around 1100AD. By 1300 huge stone walls were being built without mortar, and the fact that they still stand today is testimony to the quality of the masonry. The kingdom grew in size and power and profited from the region's gold reserves. However, most of the gold artefacts that were recovered from Great Zimbabwe a century ago were sold in South Africa and melted down, thereby destroying a wealth of treasure and historical information. This loss of artefacts, together with the lack of written records, has added mystery to this once great city, although a combination of scientific examinations and the Shona people's oral history have pieced together a basic history.

From the first thorough studies in 1905, all evidence has shown an 'unquestionably African' civilization, despite claims to the contrary. In the first half of the 15th century King Mutota increased the size of the kingdom, reaching as far as the northern and southern boundaries of modern Zimbabwe. But after the death of the king's son and successor Mutope, around 1480, the kingdom split into rival groups and Great Zimbabwe was abandoned.

NAVAL EXPLORATION AND SLAVERY

Until the 15th century, Europeans had not sailed any further than Morocco. Then, in a relatively short period, Diego Cão reached the Skeleton Coast in Namibia in 1485, Bartolomeu Dias rounded the Cape of Good Hope in 1488 and ten years later Vasco da Gama sailed around Africa to India. These three Portuguese sailors, together with countrymen who had undertaken shorter journeys before them, mapped out the vast Atlantic and Indian ocean coastlines of Africa.

This was a golden age for Portugal, whose navigation of the African coastline started an era of naval trade, but incredibly, three centuries later, major geological features of the African continent – Victoria Falls, Mount Kilimanjaro, Lake Victoria, the Ruwenzori Mountains and a chain of Rift Valley lakes – were all yet to be discovered. Even on the coast of West Africa where trading bases were being established, Europeans seldom ventured far inland. For the next few centuries Europeans were too busy with lucrative trade to do too much exploring.

Forts and castles were set up, particularly along the Gold Coast (now Ghana) from where much of West Africa's gold came. During the 16th and 17th centuries trade on the west coast concentrated largely on commodities, particularly gold and ivory, although small numbers of slaves were also taken, mainly for domestic use in Europe. However, further south the Portuguese were removing so many slaves from the region that is now Angola and Congo that by 1526 the King of Kongo wrote to his ally, John III in Lisbon, complaining of Portuguese slavers depopulating his country. But the Portuguese did not stop. In 1680 it was estimated that a million slaves had been transported from the region in the previous century.

Around this time slavery in Africa worsened substantially, with the French, British, Dutch, Germans, Spanish and Danes all joining the Portuguese in the lucrative trade in humans. European muskets traded for slaves enabled African chiefs to wage war on weaker ethnic groups, enslaving more prisoners. With other stronger groups doing the same, more muskets were needed for protection, so more people were taken. The bloody cycle, fuelled by the new need for slaves on the plantations and mines of the Americas, enslaved an estimated 10 to 12 million Africans. Two million are thought to have perished on the voyage there and unknown numbers died during battles, capture and at work in the Americas.

The vast numbers of slaves captured are incomprehensible. A more realistic view of the misery is gained by looking into the slave-holding forts and castles along the Ghanaian coast. Cells no bigger than a small bedroom held up to 200 slaves, packed so tight that many suffocated. When a boat arrived, slaves were branded with red hot irons and put on ships where conditions were often worse.

It was largely British conscience that eventually stopped the slave trade. The British Navy patrolled the Atlantic Ocean with some 20 vessels and detained over 1 300 slave ships in the 60 years after the 1807 ban on the slave trade. Some 130 000 slaves were freed, but an estimated 1.4 million had slipped through the cordon. While the trade was starting to die out in West Africa during the 1800s, it began to take off in East Africa. Early explorers followed slave routes to a hinterland devastated by the trade. In the 1860s the British Navy patrolled the Indian Ocean to catch slave ships, and in 1873 the practice was eventually banned in Zanzibar, the main slave port. In other parts of Africa it has taken much longer to abolish, with Mauritania finally outlawing it only in 1980.

EXPLORATION

The exploration of West Africa's interior had two main purposes – to find the source, course and outlet of the Niger River, and to find Timbuktu. Five centuries earlier the Moroccan traveller Ibn Battuta had commented on the ease of travel and security in the region, but the slave trade had destabilized the Sahel and bred mistrust between various tribes, and especially of Europeans. Also, modern medicines did not yet effectively control the tropical diseases that the explorers encountered.

In 1791 explorer Daniel Houghton died on the way towards the Niger River and Timbuktu. Mungo Park sailed straight past Timbuktu on the Niger River, was ambushed downstream and drowned. In 1826 Alexander Gordon Laing reached Timbuktu, which qualified him for a large cash prize as the first person to give an eye-witness report of the city. But he was murdered at the start of his return journey. The first European to claim the prize was a young independent Frenchman – René Callié – who reached the city in 1828. On a map of West African exploration, the lines marking the routes of most of the famous explorers come to a dead end, literally, because of hostility from the local people, or disease.

ABOVE *Dating back three centuries, Cape Coast Castle in Ghana is a ghastly reminder of the horrific slave trade.*

More renowned than West African explorers are the names associated with Southern and East Africa – people like Burton, Speke, Grant, Stanley, Baker and of course Livingstone. From 1848 it took just 40 years to discover virtually every major East African geological feature – Africa's three tallest mountains (Kenya, Kilimanjaro and Ruwenzori), the continent's three largest lakes (Victoria, Tanganyika and Malawi), as well as Lakes Albert and Turkana, and the source of the Nile.

Doctor David Livingstone made numerous discoveries on several journeys. Among his triumphs were the Zambezi River and Victoria Falls, as well as Lake Malawi. On an 1866 expedition the Scottish missionary-explorer set out from Quelimane (in Mozambique) to find

the source of the Nile (the 1862 discovery by John Hanning Speke was disputed). When little had been heard of Livingstone for five years, the *New York Herald* sent Henry Morton Stanley to search for him. Travelling on Arab slaving routes, Stanley found Livingstone (who was not lost) on the 10th of November 1871 at the trading town of Ujiji on the shores of Lake Tanganyika, uttering the immortal words 'Dr Livingstone, I presume'.

Although the second half of the 19th century was the period of East African discovery, settlers had been in Southern Africa for two centuries by then. Expeditions into and across the interior of Southern Africa had been made by many people, such as William Paterson and Colonel Robert Gordon who discovered the mouth of the Orange River in 1779. Early pioneer farmers were constantly expanding their boundaries from Cape Town, while the Portuguese were venturing into the interior from Mozambique. Missionary-explorers Robert Moffat and his son-in-law David Livingstone pushed further north of modern-day South African borders, as did William Burchell whose illustrations and botanical and zoological records were of great importance. Unhappy with British rule in the Cape, Boers spread north-east in what became known as the 'Great Trek'. With the discovery of gold and diamonds, further explorations of the southern region in the 19th century were largely of an entrepreneurial nature, bringing a new wave of European interest in Africa.

SCRAMBLE, COLONIALISM AND INDEPENDENCE

Africa was still recovering from the devastating slave trade when another onslaught hit the continent in what became known as the 'Scramble for Africa' where European nations raced for the best pieces of the African 'cake'. Of prime importance were points strategic

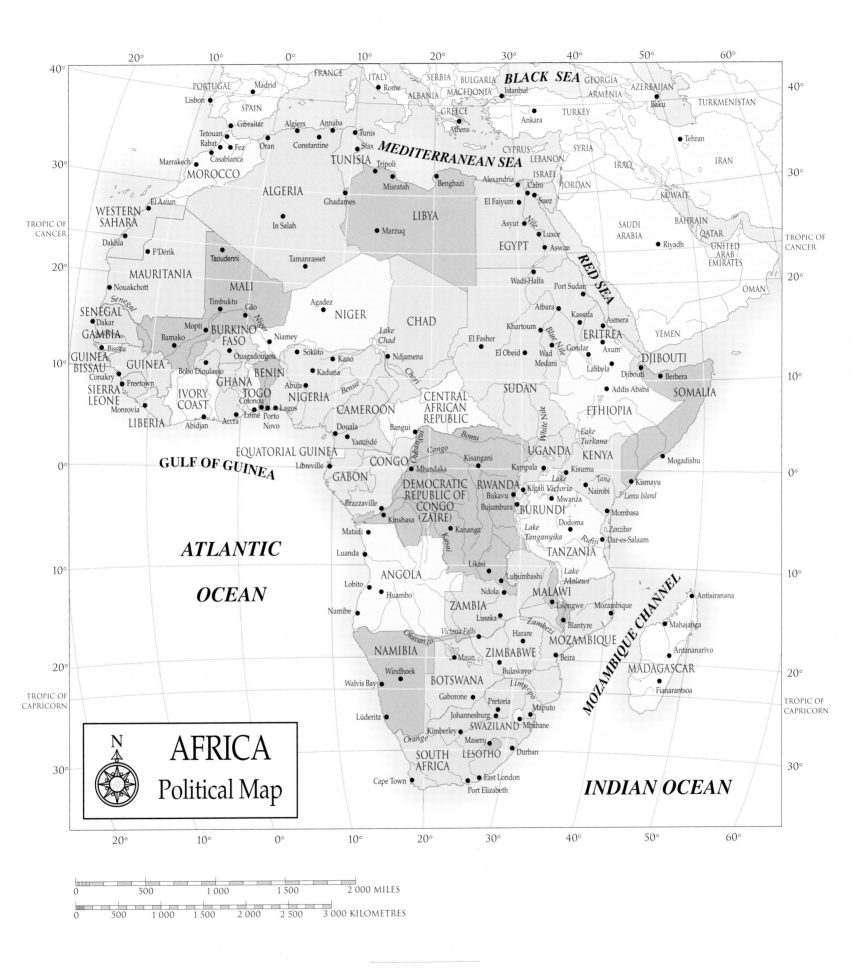

AFRICA
Political Map

to shipping – the Suez and Cape Town – as well as areas around the great rivers of the Nile, Niger, Congo and Zambezi. In 1894/95, fourteen countries met at the Berlin Conference to decide how Africa – nearly a quarter of the earth's landmass – should be shared out. No Africans were invited.

The scramble amounted to a wholesale invasion of the African continent by Europe. Across Africa minor wars broke out as Africans tried to protect their territories. Superior European firepower meant resistance to colonization was generally quickly and severely punished. In West Africa in the Ivory Coast, French soldiers would take the severed heads of freedom fighters and place them atop sharpened poles as a warning to others of what would happen if they did not bow to 'civilization'. Resistance by Herero in South West Africa (now Namibia) led to the Germans putting out an extermination order, which included women and children, resulting in the genocide of the majority of the Herero people, leaving just 15 000 wretched survivors.

Similarly, the Nama people, also of the then South West Africa, lost half of their population trying to protect their ancestral lands. Ethiopia was one of the few African kingdoms strong enough to resist colonial invaders on the battlefield. The Italians thought they were far superior (militarily and racially) so it came as a shock when their force of 19 000 soldiers was routed by the Ethiopians in just half a day with the loss of 70 percent of their men.

While most of the unrest during the scramble was between colonists and Africans, in South Africa the discovery of gold and diamonds

LEFT *Body scarification, body painting, lip piercing and chipping teeth to sharp points are means of beautification used by Pygmies.*

upped the stakes for control between the British and the Boers, eventually escalating to what became known as the Boer War.

The boundaries formed by the colonial powers, after bartering and trade-offs, were ridiculous in the extreme. Cabinda, part of Angola, is still separated from the rest of the country by the country and river of Congo. Namibia has an appendage called the Caprivi Strip, a long, narrow piece of land that stretches eastwards for several hundred kilometres between Botswana and Angola. Germany received the Caprivi Strip and a small rock in the North Sea called Heligoland (unimportant at the time but strategic during the World Wars) from the British in exchange for the islands of Zanzibar and Pemba (off Tanzania) and recognition of their Ugandan boundaries. Even today several countries (Nigeria and Cameroon, Libya and Chad, Ethiopia and Somalia) have ongoing disputes over boundaries set by the colonials.

Enticed with a hint of freedom, many Africans were recruited or conscripted to fight in World War II. But after the war freedom never came, and some of the returned soldiers became disgruntled with their treatment at the hands of the Allies and independence movements gained momentum. The colonial view was that independence in most cases was inevitable, but Africa was not yet ready (in many cases 'not ready' meant there was not yet a level of disruption that seriously threatened the colonialists' control). But many countries were unprepared for independence, with few qualified or educated Africans (Congo [Kinshasa] had a mere 12 university graduates at independence), and with several economies relying heavily on a single commodity.

When the various African countries became independent, many European colonialists left en masse, fearing retaliation for previous ill-treatment of indigenous Africans, but with a few exceptions their fears were largely unfounded. However, the 1960s and 1970s were a period of coups and dictatorships in much of Africa. Countries with a largely untrained and illiterate populous had little chance of advancing and governments sometimes floundered, often resulting in power transferring to military strongmen. While there have been countless coups in Africa since the 1960s wave of independence, there have also been numerous wars, some for independence, but the majority were due to civil unrest, with only a few fought between two or more countries.

In recent times many civil wars, some that have been running for decades, have come to an end. All African countries now have independence from their former colonial powers, although a few still seem to be caught in a cycle of going from dictator to dictator. Even today traditionalism plays an active and often destructive part in politics. But democracy and stability are becoming more common across larger regions, even in previously troubled areas.

PEOPLE AND CULTURE

No continent is more diverse in its people than Africa, with a staggering 2 000 ethnic groups inhabiting the continent, most with their own language or dialect. Some are known for their height, such as Kenya's Samburu, and others like the Pygmies are known for their short stature; there are those who are very dark and others who are extremely light-skinned.

While physical difference may only be skin-deep, it is in individual cultures that distinctions are more pronounced. Some ethnic groups have only recently left the Stone Age for the Iron Age, while others still practise blood sacrifices, but many of these societies are advanced in conservation, healing, art and social cohesion of their group or extended family – aspects in which many 'developed' societies are failing.

Many other ethnic groups have migrated to Africa over the centuries. Among them are people of Asian origin, particularly from India, who inhabit the east and southern regions, and large Arab populations across North Africa and on the East African coast who have, in many places, fully integrated with local populations. Several million people of European origins live in Southern Africa, although few would consider themselves anything but African.

The vast majority of indigenous Africans can be divided into four distinct language families (phylum). The Afro-Asiatic group dominates North Africa and the Horn of Africa (Africa's eastern protrusion consisting of Somalia, and usually also Djibouti and Ethiopia), while the Niger-Kordofanian phylum covers most of sub-Saharan Africa. A third group, Nilo-Saharan, covers the central Sahel and parts of East Africa while the final distinct phylum, making up less than one percent of Africa's overall population, are the Khoisan of Southern Africa. Even languages within the same phylum can be as disparate as English and Hindi.

The Afro-Asiatic phylum has over 100 million speakers, with Arabic being one of the most widely spoken languages in Africa. This group also encompasses Hebrew, and the widely spoken Amharic language of Ethiopia, one of Africa's few indigenous written languages with its own alphabet. Another member of this group is Berber, comprising many related groups across North Africa including Tuareg nomads in the Sahara Desert. Distantly related to Berber but with no modern equivalent is Ancient Egyptian. Other Afro-Asiatic languages are found around the Horn of Africa and as far south as Tanzania.

The Niger-Kordofanian phylum contains the small Kordofanian subgroup with a mere 30 or so languages. The Niger-Congo branch is the most widespread language group and contains the large group of related Bantu languages. Bantu-speakers are thought to have spread out from the Nigeria/Cameroon region around 3 000 years ago, reaching Kenya by 100AD and South Africa by 300AD, largely absorbing or bypassing hunter-gatherer people they met on the way. Spreading over such a vast area, not only into habitable but also into relatively hostile regions, the Bantu-speaking peoples are one of Africa's most successful groups.

The Nilo-Saharan phylum dominates the region around Chad and extends from here to oases in southern Libya, the Nile in southern Egypt and west to the Songhay people of Mali. In East Africa this group is particularly well represented in Kenya, where various groups make up over 90 percent of the population.

The fourth distinct language group, Khoisan, is largely restricted to a small group of people in Southern Africa. Khoisan languages are notable for their 'clicks' of which there are many different types, though the untrained ear will struggle to pick up differences. The Khoisan group includes the San (Bushmen) who in the past were persecuted by various South African groups, forcing them into the arid regions around the Kalahari Desert. An estimated 200 000 were killed, and even today their numbers have recovered to just 50 000. Other Khoisan are the Khoi, who are thought to be San who changed their hunter-gatherer lifestyle and took to cattle and sheep farming, and a group (now vanished) known as the 'Strandlopers' (meaning beachcombers) who specialized as coastal hunter-gatherers.

As well as the four main African language families, many foreign languages are also spoken. Most countries have inherited a

ABOVE *The majority of Mali's cliff-dwelling Dogon people cling to their traditional spiritual world and animist beliefs.*
OPPOSITE *A peanut vendor in Tanzania carries her wares on her head – a common sight throughout Africa.*

language from their former European colonial power, particularly English and French, but there are also other languages, such as various pidgins and Creoles, which are a mix of European and African languages.

There are few countries where the whole population can communicate in the same language, but it is not uncommon for people without a formal education to speak three or four languages fluently. Only Somalia, and the small countries of Lesotho and Swaziland, have a population of a single ethnic group (Somalis, Basotho and Swazi respectively). In a few other countries a single group makes up 75 percent or more of the population, such as

the Shona of Zimbabwe and the Hutu in both Burundi and Rwanda. At the other end of the spectrum is the Democratic Republic of Congo (formerly Zaïre) with well over 200 different ethnic groups, most with their own languages.

A few regions are notable for the diversity of origins of their people. South Africa stands out as an example of this, and although it may contain comparatively few ethnic groups, their backgrounds are some of the most varied. Perhaps the most obvious South African group are the Afrikaners whose history of a pioneering heritage goes back several centuries. Their language, Afrikaans, is spoken only in Southern Africa. Not quite as numerous are the some two million South Africans of British descent, many of whom can trace their African heritage to the British colonization of the Cape in the early 1800s.

Other South African minorities include Portuguese, Germans, Dutch, Greeks, Italians and French. Like many countries on the Indian Ocean, South Africa has a substantial Indian population of around a million people, many whose families originally came here to work on the sugar plantations in the 1800s.

The Coloured people of South Africa number around four million, a significant minority of which are Cape Malays: Muslim people descended from slaves from the Dutch East Indies (Indonesia) who arrived when Cape Town was a stop-over between Europe and the East Indies. Like the Afrikaners, this group has developed a unique culture.

The majority of South Africans are Bantu-speaking. Groups include the Basotho, Tswana, Swazi, Tsonga and Ndebele, who are all found in neighbouring countries as well. Other groups include the Pedi and the country's two largest groups, the Zulu and Xhosa, who both speak Nguni languages, a subgroup of Bantu.

The Zulu have a proud history of warfare, especially by renowned warrior king, Shaka, who revolutionized hand-to-hand combat with great success. As well as defeating African groups, the Zulu also won battles against the British and Boers before finally succumbing to superior weaponry.

The Xhosa have several distinct subgroups, with many living a traditional lifestyle herding cattle, and revering their ancestors and spirits. Their ways are changing (like all South African ethnic groups, there are many Xhosa who are very urbanized) but spiritual healers and herbalists are still held in high regard.

Another ethnic group, the Venda, are of slightly more obscure origin. They have strong traditions in metalwork and pottery and also have a strong link with their spirits.

Although some Bantu-speaking peoples arrived in South Africa 17 centuries ago, the earliest inhabitants, dating back thousands of years, are the Khoisan. They, together with all of South Africa's ethnic groups, form a spectrum of distinct and different people who are worthy of the new South Africa's self-appointed title 'rainbow nation'.

East Africa's ethnic groups also have a diverse range of backgrounds. The region, and particularly the Rift Valley, has been called the 'cradle of mankind', from where not only Africa's but also the world's earliest inhabitants are believed to have come. Representatives of the four major African language families can all be found in East Africa.

Over 3 000 kilometres (1 864 miles) from the Khoisan people of Southern Africa, two isolated groups in Tanzania also speak 'click' languages, and are believed to be linked to the Khoisan. The Sandawe, and the small Hadza group who live not far from the early man sites of Laetoli and Olduvai, have until recent times also been hunter-gatherers.

Another of East Africa's earliest peoples are the Pygmies whose eastern limits are the forests of Uganda. Small numbers also survive in Rwanda and Burundi, but over 99 percent of these country's populations are either the generally short Hutu or the tall Tutsi, who for around four decades have been involved in a brutal and bloody power struggle.

In contrast to the polarized peoples of Burundi and Rwanda, neighbouring Tanzania has over 120 different ethnic groups, mainly of Bantu-speaking origin. In Kenya the largest single ethnic group are the Kikuyu, but the vast majority of the country's people are from the Nilo-Saharan phylum – Maasai, Samburu, Turkana and Luo to name a few. On the East African coast a mix of Arab and African has formed the Swahili people and culture.

Thought to have arrived earlier than either the Bantu-speakers or Nilo-Saharan groups are people from the Cushitic branch of the Afro-Asiatic phylum – the Rendille and Galla, who came south from Ethiopia. Also Cushitic, and covering much of the Horn of Africa, including eastern Kenya and all of Somalia, are the Somali people. The Somalis are also found in Ethiopia, a land of diverse peoples where, as opposed to the single language of Somalia, over 70 languages are spoken. The varied cultures of the Ethiopian peoples range from different animist groups, including the very small Karo group of just a few hundred people in the Omo Valley, to several million Amhara with a 30-century-history of a monarchy and 16 centuries of indigenous Christianity, to the fiercely independent Muslim Afar, or Danakil, nomads of the harsh Danakil Desert.

Parts of West Africa have perhaps the greatest number of ethnic groups, especially in the Nigeria/Cameroon region where the three biggest language groups again coincide. This is also the region where Bantu-speakers are thought to have originated from. Cameroon has well over 100 ethnic groups and Nigeria around 250, but as well as numerous small groups, there are also some of Africa's largest groups present. Just 10 groups make up the majority of Nigeria's population of over

Tuareg nomads of the Sahara Desert, although Muslims like almost all North Africans, are different in their customs. With Tuaregs, who are part of the Berber group, it is the men who are fully veiled with only their eyes showing, while women will sometimes wear an open headcloth. Tuaregs are not the only nomad groups of the Sahara. Arab Bedouin and related Arab groups like the Baggara (Baqqara) of Sudan and Chad, who number several million, have lived in the Sahara for several centuries as nomadic or semi-nomadic cattle herders.

In Egypt the vast majority of the population are descendants of the Ancient Egyptians, who are speculated to be of Berber origin, with influences from other Africans further south as well as from people from the Middle East.

CULTURE

What some people perceive to be evil beliefs or witchcraft often have important roles in African societies. The Bemba of Zambia believe it is lucky to find a bee's nest of honey, and very lucky to find two. But to find three is witchcraft and must be punished. This belief is a method of conservation to preserve the continual supply of honey. Likewise, some Pygmy clans who must control the population in their fragile rainforest environment do not allow sex while a mother is breast-feeding as they believe it can poison the baby through the mother's milk. As breast-feeding can last up to three years, this is an effective method of birth control.

In certain societies, unusual events like earthquakes, disease epidemics, droughts, floods or plagues of insects are thought to be punishment from the spirits who may need appeasing with a sacrifice. A human culprit with whom the spirits are angry may be found – perhaps a thief or someone who has broken a social custom – and may be required to make a

100 million people, including the Hausa from the Afro-Asiatic language group who number around 20 million. Often associated with the Hausa (after they conquered them in the 19th century) are the Fulani, originally semi-nomadic cattle herders but now spread over more than 10 Sahel countries. Various and sometimes isolated groups of Fulani are gradually forming different cultures under different names including Peul, Wodaabe (Bororo), Fulbe and Fula. Large ethnic groups from the Niger-Kordofanian language group include the Yoruba who live in south-west Nigeria around Lagos and Ibadan (West Africa's two largest cities), and the Ibo (Igbo)

who live in eastern Nigeria and tried unsuccessfully to break away from Nigeria in the late 1960s as the Republic of Biafra.

Compared to the ethnic complexity of Africa south of the Sahara, in the north the situation is much simpler. Across Morocco, Algeria, Tunisia and Libya virtually all of the population are either Berber or Arab, or a mixture of both. The Moroccans have sometimes been referred to as Moors. Previously this somewhat inexact term has been used for various different groups up to, and including, all Muslims right across North Africa and Spain, but nowadays is a common term for Mauritanians of Moroccan descent.

blood sacrifice of an animal. In this way the sacrifice can serve several purposes: it bonds individuals to society's rules, it is a punishment, and it could benefit the community who may share the animal after it has been sacrificed.

Many traditional religions, often referred to as animism (from the Latin *anima* meaning 'breath' or 'soul'), believe their ancestors are an intermediary step between themselves and god. Creation myths are common and not dissimilar in many ways to the Christian belief of Adam and Eve. A single Supreme Being and the deceased going to heaven or the spirit world are other parallels that many African religions have with Christianity.

Animist religions, including voodoo that was taken to the Americas by slaves, are often labelled as inherently dark and evil, but in many traditional religions spirits are neither good nor evil but neutral unless someone has done something to upset the balance. In this case diviners, witch doctors or sorcerers may be used to appease a spirit or remove a curse.

While traditional medicine and herbalists are beginning to be accepted as a legitimate practise by Western medical experts (and have provided the world with important medicines such as cures for some forms of cancer), spiritual healing is still little understood. But in sub-Saharan Africa it is common knowledge that people who think they are cursed can 'will' themselves to die, while the belief of patients in a spiritual healer's ability to cure them or remove a curse can have a profound effect on their recovery. Many traditional beliefs are being lost as Islam and Christianity are adopted across Africa, but new religions often become an addition, not a replacement, to animism.

Islam completely dominates North Africa, having arrived there over a thousand years ago, and is also particularly strong across the Sahel region, around the Horn of Africa and down the east coast. In other areas Christian missions, mainly in the last 150 years, have sought converts with varying degrees of success. Some countries, like Nigeria and Sudan, are divided regionally with Muslims in the north and Christians in the south. Ethiopia has roughly even numbers of Muslims and Christians with a sizable animist minority. As well as Ethiopia's Orthodox Christian Church being connected to Judaism, the country also has a small group of African Jews, the Falashas.

OPPOSITE *Old sacrifices hang on an altar hut of the Hogon (village spiritual leader) in the cliffside village of Ireli in Mali.*
BELOW *An Ethiopian nun adorned with a necklace of amber; this consists of pieces of fossilized tree resin that are highly prized by many African cultures.*

The continent has an enormous variety of religions, from the earliest versions of Christianity, Islam and animism, to virtually all modern forms of Christianity, as well as Asian religions that are practised almost exclusively by Asian ethnic groups. The specific religion that an African ethnic group adheres to largely affects the rest of their culture – its music, adornments and particularly its visual art.

ART, MUSIC AND ADORNMENTS

African art has largely developed without outside influence, but it has influenced outsiders, like Modigliani who collected African art. The most prominent facet of African art is probably mask-making. Masks are seldom made just for their aesthetic qualities, but are used in traditional ceremonies and dance, usually to represent a spirit or ancestor while disguising the human wearer. Wooden mask-making is widespread throughout sub-Saharan Africa, but is particularly prominent in West Africa and the Central African rainforests.

Like masks, wooden figurines are a popular art form and are often part of everyday life with connections to the spirits. People like the Dogon of Mali live in a world where virtually every object has a connection to the spirit world, so items like wooden doors and locks are all carved with representations of ancestors. As the majority of traditional artworks across Africa are in daily use, or at least regular use, and are made of wood, there are few pieces left that are more than a century old.

Contrasting to the temporary nature of wooden carvings are rock paintings and etchings, many of which are several thousand years old. While most wooden masks and statuettes represent the human form, animals as well as humans are common in rock art, examples of which can be found particularly in the Sahara Desert and in Southern Africa.

Dating back hundreds of years is another form of painting – unique Ethiopian religious illustrations, many of which can still be found inside many churches and monasteries. South Africa's Ndebele are also renowned for their brightly coloured art work, seen as vivid geometric designs on their houses.

New art forms have also become popular, such as in Zimbabwe where Shona sculpture has been produced in the last few decades. The stylized stone sculptures are purely artistic, unlike much traditional art where the use or purpose of an object is important. In East Africa cloth batiks have become fashionable, as have carvings known as 'Makonde' statues, or 'family trees', originally made by the Makonde people of the border region of Mozambique and Tanzania. A large variety of art is originating from western

Nigeria in the Ibadan and Oshogbo regions, including batiks, paintings and montages. Although non-traditional art forms, they are highly influenced by the Yoruba people's animist religion which still prevails over Christianity and Islam. Considering Nigeria's long history of bronze, iron and terracotta artworks, some dating back over 2 000 years, it is not surprising that a number of Africa's most renowned artists come from this region.

Where Islam dominates in the Sahel region, and in North Africa, art has taken on different forms in that religion bars reproducing living creatures. To a large extent architecture is artistic, seen particularly in the elaborate mud mosques of the Sahel and detailed tiled mosaics of North African mosques. Morocco has become known for many of its crafts, including carpet-making, leatherware, and

ABOVE *Rock etchings in the Sahara Desert near Taghit, Algeria, date back as far as 5000BC when the Sahara was much greener.*

silver and brass work. Ancient Egypt is also known for its many and varied artworks, ranging from giant statues like those of the Sphinx and Ramses II, to paintings and gold statues of the pharaohs.

Just as art is often integrated into African religions and social structure, so too is traditional music and dance. Specific songs and dances often form part of social ceremonies that incorporate a particular event for a village, be it harvest, coming of the rains, a marriage, death or promotion of an age-based group to its next level. In these ceremonies, traditional religions and beliefs are strongly involved and myths and legends are acted out in song and dance, as well as in traditional storytelling. Across Africa most ethnic groups have their storytellers, but for the Somali people it is their poets that are renowned, and have been since they were described by early explorers. These oral traditions are paramount to a group's cultural identity and until relatively recently, they have taken the place of written history.

Musically Africa is probably best known for its drums, of which there are numerous types, including stretched animal skins over hollow wood or gourds, hollowed out logs without skin, as well as xylophone-type percussion instruments.

When it comes to string instruments, Africa has a large array, including the large 21-stringed kora (harp-lute) of West Africa and the very large Luo lyre of Kenya. The many Ethiopian stringed instruments include the masinqo – a single stringed instrument played with a bow. In West Africa, Fulani shepherds are known for the music of their reed flutes, as are shepherds in Ethiopia, where there are various traditional wind instruments.

While music plays an important part in a culture's ceremonies and even a large part in everyday life, adornments are even more ingrained into many cultures' identities. Specific ethnic groups have their own style of jewellery, or dress, or body scarification. In Niger and Ethiopia silver hand-made crosses of various designs, usually worn as pendants, signify specific towns. Across Africa, but particularly in Sudan and West Africa, facial scarification signifies ethnic identity, while in some remote parts of Ethiopia scarification on the arms and legs (in groups like the Mursi), or on the jewellery of some groups, signifies how many enemies a man has killed – the number determining his social status. Also in Ethiopia,

in the remote Omo Valley, Surma women, along with Sara women of Chad, still wear enormous clay lip plates and ear plates, a tradition thought by some to originate from the slave trading days when women tried to make themselves unattractive to slavers.

Some Ndebele women in South Africa still wear layers of thick metal rings around their necks. Several groups stretch their earlobes but the Maasai of East Africa are particularly renowned for this. The tall, lean Maasai are also prominent because of their brightly coloured beaded jewellery (similar to that of other Kenyan groups such as the El Molo, Samburu, Turkana and Pokot) and their robes, usually bright red for Kenyan Maasai. Known for their ear decorations are the Peul women of West Africa who wear fluted saucer-sized gold earrings for adornment and as a status symbol.

For several ethnic groups, including some Pygmy clans, chipping their teeth to sharp points is seen as a sign of beauty. Body painting is common across sub-Saharan Africa, but rather than day-to-day use, it is done more for special events like marriages, circumcision ceremonies and funerals. However, some peoples like the Himba of Namibia will almost permanently cover their skin with butterfat and ochre, which serves as a sunscreen and moisturizer in their hot, dry environment, and the Dinka of Sudan mask themselves in white ash, which protects them from mosquitoes.

In places where there is an Arab influence, women sometimes have intricate patterns painted on their hands and feet with henna. It is not uncommon for women in the Christian highlands of Ethiopia to boast facial tattoos, usually in the form of a cross, as do some Berber women of North Africa.

These adornments and markings, usually carried out as a trial of endurance and pain, bond a people together as a cohesive group.

Music, art, myths and legends combine with religion to give an encompassing identity. The enormous differences in these identities and cultures help to structure various societies in often difficult and harsh environments.

GEOGRAPHY AND CLIMATE

The African continent lies on a single tectonic plate, but that plate is slowly splitting in two, continuing to form what is perhaps the world's most important geological feature – the Great Rift. Along the Rift the earth's crust is bending and fracturing, creating a scar so large it can easily be seen from the moon with the naked eye. Nearly every major natural landmark on the eastern side of Africa has directly or indirectly been caused by the Great Rift, including the continent's highest mountain, largest lake, its lowest depression, and sources for the world's longest river.

Stretching approximately 7 000 kilometres (4 300 miles) from the Indian Ocean off Mozambique, the Great Rift travels up the length of East Africa through to Lebanon in the Middle East. In places the stretched crust has fractured, resulting in volcanoes and uplifting of blocks of the earth's crust by internal pressures. Where East Africa and the Horn of Africa continue to break away from the rest of the continent, the Rift has caused trenches and these have filled with water to become some of the world's deepest and longest lakes. Lake Tanganyika (Africa's deepest and longest) is over 650 kilometres (400 miles) long and nearly 1 500 metres (4 900 feet) deep, putting the lake bed around 700 metres (2 300 feet) below sea level. Its surface area is larger than Israel and it holds so much water that it could keep the Niagara Falls in full flood for over 70 years.

Though not quite as deep, and slightly shorter than Lake Tanganyika, Lake Malawi is still a substantial lake at some 568 kilometres

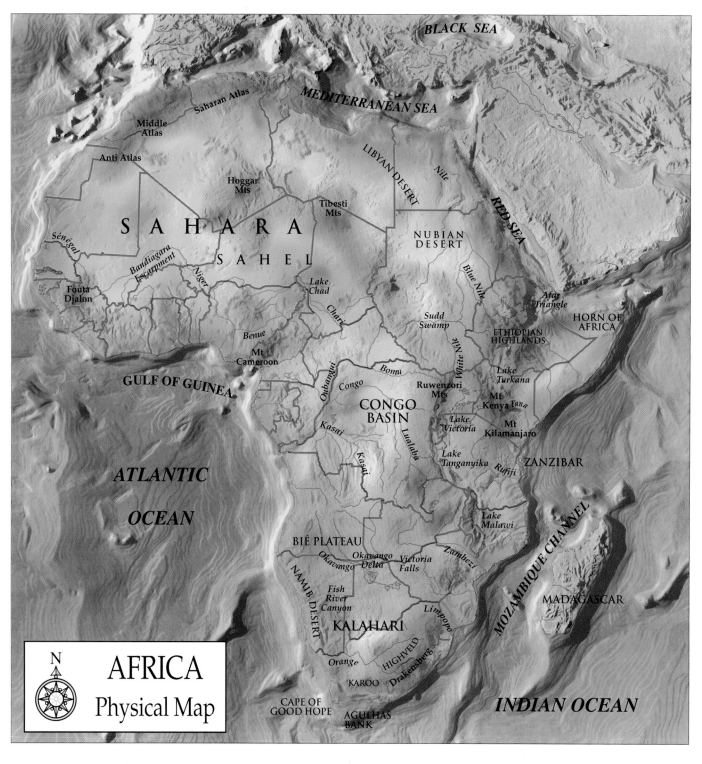

BLACK SEA

MEDITERRANEAN SEA

Saharan Atlas

Middle
Atlas

Anti Atlas

LIBYAN DESERT

Nile

Hoggar
Mts

Tibesti
Mts

RED SEA

S A H A R A

NUBIAN
DESERT

Sénégal

S A H E L

*Bandiagara
Escarpment*

Niger

Lake
Chad

Blue Nile

*Afar
Triangle*

Fouta
Djalon

Chari

Sudd
Swamp

ETHIOPIAN
HIGHLANDS

HORN OF
AFRICA

Benue

Mt
Cameroon

GULF OF GUINEA

Oubangui

Bomu

White Nile

Ruwenzori
Mts

Lake
Turkana

Congo

CONGO
BASIN

Mt
Kenya

Tana

Kasai

Lake
Victoria

Mt
Kilamanjaro

Luataba

ATLANTIC

Kasai

Lake
Tanganyika

Rufiji

ZANZIBAR

OCEAN

Lake
Malawi

MOZAMBIQUE CHANNEL

BIÉ PLATEAU

Okavango

Okavango
Delta

Victoria
Falls

Zambezi

MADAGASCAR

NAMIB DESERT

Fish
River
Canyon

Limpopo

KALAHARI

Orange

HIGHVELD

Drakensberg

KAROO

CAPE OF
GOOD HOPE

AGULHAS
BANK

INDIAN OCEAN

N

AFRICA
Physical Map

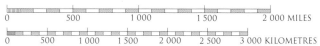

0   500   1 000   1 500   2 000 MILES

0   500   1 000   1 500   2 000   2 500   3 000 KILOMETRES

(353 miles) long and 23 300 square kilometres (8 996 square miles) in surface area. It forms part of the Western Rift chain that starts with the lower Zambezi River and carries on in an intermittent trough through the major lakes of Malawi, Tanganyika, Kivu and Edward, as well as many smaller lakes, ending in Uganda's Lake Albert at its Nile outlet.

As well as lakes, the Western Rift has created the Virunga Mountains in eastern Congo (Kinshasa) – a chain of active volcanoes that regularly erupt, showing that the forces which created the Rift are still at work. In the same region the Rift has also given rise to the Ruwenzori Mountains. Being at the edge of the equatorial rainforest, humid air rising over the Ruwenzoris causes a regional rainfall of up to 3 000 millimetres (118 inches) of rain per year.

In contrast to the Western Rift's deep lakes, the Eastern Rift's chain of lakes are generally very shallow. This causes great evaporation and a high level of minerals in the remaining water. One of these shallow alkaline lakes – Kenya's Lake Magadi – is possibly the most mineral-laden lake in the world, the minerals forming a crust so strong that trucks can be driven on it.

Other alkaline (or soda) lakes breed algae on which flamingos thrive. The flamingos can be found along the Eastern Rift's string of lakes that starts in Tanzania and runs all the way up through Kenya and Ethiopia. Other features caused by the Rift along the way are the massive Ngorongoro Crater and several other volcanoes in the vicinity, including Sadiman which spewed ash 3.6 million years ago, thus preserving the world's oldest humanoid footprints at Laetoli.

Although many features are not located directly on the Great Rift, they have been caused by it. The great scarps on the eastern side of the Ethiopian Highlands mark the Rift, but the rest of the Highlands continue for

several hundred kilometres west. Uplifting and lava build-up, almost 4 kilometres (2.5 miles) thick, has given the Ethiopian Highlands such a high altitude (up to 4 620 metres [15 157 feet] at Mount Ras Dashen) that they have a wet, cool climate. This wet climate has helped to create Lake Tana, the source of the Blue Nile.

The major source of the White Nile, Lake Victoria, is not directly on the Rift either, although it was indirectly caused by the Rift's internal pressures warping the earth's crust. With a surface area greater than the combined total of the nearby countries of Burundi and Rwanda, Lake Victoria is also large enough to create its own climatic conditions, with higher rainfall along parts of its shoreline than in surrounding areas. With Lake Victoria as a centrepiece, the Western Rift curls away to the south and the Eastern Rift to the north.

The volcanoes of mounts Kilimanjaro and Kenya, Africa's two highest mountains, are both caused by the Rift but are well off its

ABOVE *Virtually on the equator in East Africa, the snowy peaks of the Ruwenzori Mountains defy the hot, dry images of Africa.*

course. Again these mountains have their own climatic conditions, quite different from the surrounding countryside. They are both high enough to have permanent glacial ice and their altitudes create clouds as warm air, forced to rise and cool, condenses.

Often shrouded in mist, these mountains receive heavy rainfall, although the peak of Kilimanjaro (where there is permanent snow and ice) is often above the clouds and receives so little rain that it could be classified as a desert. Mount Kilimanjaro's neighbour, the 4 800-metre-high (15 748 feet) volcanic Mount Meru, is Africa's fifth highest mountain, but is thought to have been higher until a massive eruption blew the top kilometre off the mountain around 250 000 years ago.

Earth movements as far away as Botswana have also been attributed to internal pressures caused by the Great Rift. In the past the course of the Zambezi River has changed – it once flowed into Africa's biggest lake in what is now the Kalahari Desert. Similarly, Botswana's Okavango River used to flow south to the Limpopo River on the border with South Africa, but uplifting caused by pressure from the Rift now means the Okavango forms an inland delta and comes to a dead-end.

BELOW *The world's largest desert, the Sahara, also boasts the world's largest sand dunes, which reach 430 metres (1 410 feet).*

Through its drainage patterns the Rift has an effect on three of Africa's major river systems – the Zambezi, Congo and Nile. Lake Malawi drains into the Indian Ocean via the Shire and Zambezi rivers. To the north, Lake Tanganyika's intermittent outlet, the Lukuga River, crosses the continent to the Atlantic Ocean via the Congo River.

As little as 40 kilometres (25 miles) from Lake Tanganyika, a small spring in Burundi marks the southernmost source of the Nile. This flows into Lake Victoria, which instead of flowing to the Indian Ocean less than 700 kilometres (440 miles) away as may be expected, flows thousands of kilometres to the north into the Mediterranean Sea.

From Lake Victoria the river is called the Victoria Nile, then from Lake Albert, the Albert Nile, and after the Sudanese border until Khartoum where it meets the Blue Nile, it is variously described as Bahr el Jebel or White Nile (Nil el Abyad). From Khartoum to the Mediterranean it is simply known as the Nile. Much of the flow of the Victoria/Albert/White Nile (usually collectively called the White Nile) never reaches the Mediterranean. It comes to the impenetrable obstacle of the Sudd (which means 'obstacle').

Here the White Nile spreads out into a vast swamp the size of England, where most of its water is lost to evaporation. The Sudd is one of the world's most inhospitable places

for humans, but it is perfect for some animals, including crocodile, hippopotamus and over 60 mosquito species. A rich variety of birdlife lives among the Sudd's ever-changing floating islands of papyrus, water hyacinth and other attractive aquatic vegetation.

Where the Nile finally meets the sea after 6 670 kilometres (4 144 miles), it forms a large, fan-shaped delta. The name 'delta' is thought to have first been used for the Nile after the Greeks saw the similarity between its shape and their letter Δ (delta). Millennia of annual floods have fertilized the delta with Nile silt, providing Egypt with approximately 80 percent of its fertile land. In-between the delta and the Sudd, the world's largest desert competes with the world's longest river. The Nile makes little impression on the Sahara, but the Sahara imposes itself, pushing to within metres of the Nile in places.

Nearly 4 000 kilometres (2 485 miles) to the west, the Sahara does the same to the Niger River, as if it was trying to strangle the river between Timbuktu and Gão. Upstream from Timbuktu the Niger has a 400-kilometre-long (250 mile) inland delta. Although not on the same scale as the Sudd, a vast area is covered by annual floods. Where the Niger meets the sea, its delta is even bigger, forming streams, rivers, estuaries and swamps that spread out over 200 kilometres (125 miles) of coastline. Much of the Niger's waters rise in the Fouta Djalon, a highlands in Guinea and one of West Africa's few mountainous areas.

As well as imposing on the Nile and Niger rivers, from November to February the Sahara has an effect on the whole of West Africa. A hot, dry wind called the harmattan produces a dusty haze across much of the region. North Africa receives similar winds from the Sahara in April and May, which are variously called the Sirocco, Sahali and in Egypt, the Khamsin.

Deep in the Sahara a dramatically shaped volcanic massif – the Tibesti Mountains – rises to Emi Koussi, at 3 415 metres (11 204 feet) the Sahara's highest peak. To the west are the similar desert mountain regions of Aïr and Hoggar which rise to nearly 2 000 and 3 000 metres (6 561 and 9 842 feet) respectively. Higher still at 4 000 metres (13 123 feet), but right on the coast, is Mount Cameroon. At just 4 degrees from the equator, humid tropical air is blown straight from the sea to high altitude. The result is one of the wettest locations on earth with an astounding 10 000 millimetres (394 inches) of rain per year. Mount Cameroon is part of a volcanic chain that starts hundreds of kilometres away in the Gulf of Guinea before forming a line of volcanoes, crater lakes and volcanic plugs to the north-east virtually all the way to Lake Chad, which lies in the semi-arid Sahel region (meaning 'shore').

Outside of the Rift, Lake Chad is one of the few large natural lakes in Africa. Despite its size and intermittent position as fourth largest lake in Africa (behind lakes Tanganyika, Malawi and Victoria), it does not hold much water. With a maximum depth of just 7 metres (23 feet) and no outlet, Lake Chad loses an enormous amount of water to evaporation, fluctuating between 10 and 25 thousand square kilometres (3 861 and 9 653 square miles) in size.

From the Sahel region, both precipitation and vegetation increase towards the west coast and the equator. The equatorial region of Central Africa is dominated by the Congo Basin – an area where dense rainforest is cut by a myriad large rivers. Some are kilometres wide and over 1 000 kilometres (600 miles) long, and are merely sub-tributaries of even bigger tributaries of the vast Congo River.

Straddling the equator, the central Congo Basin receives more rain than anywhere else in Africa, except for isolated high altitude areas.

Rain falls year-round and over 30 percent of days have thunder storms. So immense is the catchment for the Congo River that at various times it receives rain from both northern and southern wet seasons, largely cancelling out any extremely low or high river levels.

These rainy seasons follow what is known as the inter-tropical convergence zone, a zone where seasonal winds meet each other, forcing damp air upwards into clouds. The zone oscillates, approximately following the longest day so that it is in the north around the June summer solstice and furthest south during the December summer solstice, passing over the equator around the equinoxes. The Congo's tributaries collect from these varying rainy seasons, including the 2 000-kilometre-long (1 200 miles) Ubangui-Uele River in the north, and the Kasai River which feeds from the Angolan plateau to the south.

The Angolan highlands are a watershed with rivers of 1 000 kilometres (620 miles) long or more, travelling in different directions and flowing into the Atlantic Ocean, the Kasai/Congo system, the Indian Ocean via the Zambezi River, and the Kalahari Desert via the Okavango Delta. Across the border in the far north-west corner of Zambia is the source of the Zambezi River – a small spring that flows 2 700 kilometres (1 678 miles) to the sea. It is most spectacular at Victoria Falls, where at its peak the equivalent of five Olympic-sized swimming pools of water per second plunge over a bluff that is about twice as high and twice as long as America's Niagara Falls.

Contrasting with the Zambezi's abundance of water are Southern Africa's deserts. The Namib Desert stretches along almost 2 000 kilometres (1 200 miles) of coastline, leaving the shoreline bleak and barren with barely a shred of greenery. For approximately 1 600 kilometres (1 000 miles) between the Kunene and Orange rivers – the full length of Namibia – no permanent rivers pass through the Namib to reach the coast. Considering its length, the Namib is very narrow, seldom reaching more than 150 kilometres (95 miles) inland. The Benguela Ocean current brings regular fog and mist to the Namib Desert, and sand from the Orange River to form large orange dunes that in places rise straight out of the Atlantic Ocean.

Much of Southern Africa is very dry, and except for a brief section of the Okavango River where it crosses the Caprivi Strip, Namibia's only permanent rivers are all on its borders and shared with its neighbours. Botswana is in a similar situation, again except for the Okavango River. Most of Botswana is covered by the Kalahari ('wilderness') Desert which also touches on all neighbouring countries. The Kalahari is a vast, flat region about the size of France, much of which is covered with patchy, dry grass and scrub.

To the south is another dry, barren region – South Africa's Karoo. The endless plains and rugged mountain ranges of the Karoo (meaning 'thirstland') cover a massive region larger than Germany. Marking the southern edge of the Karoo, and following a course roughly parallel to the coast, are the Cape ranges, created by pressures so large that they have caused the African continent to fold upwards. Like the Drakensberg to the north-east, the Cape ranges are large enough to cause their own weather patterns, and are largely responsible for the Karoo's lack of rain. Like many African mountains, they give rise to a 'rain shadow'. Moist air is forced upwards over the ranges and it cools and condenses, causing clouds and rain (watering the lush Garden Route that nestles between the mountain and the sea). The air that passes just over the ranges contains less moisture and is even less likely to produce rain as it lowers in altitude and warms up.

At the southern tip of the continent, Cape Town in South Africa receives less than 1 000 millimetres (40 inches) of rain per year. This mainly falls in winter, while summers are warm and dry. Contrasting to this is the country's city of Johannesburg which, because of its inland location, gets the majority of its rain in the summer. Cape Town's climate is comparable to some Mediterranean countries, which have a similar latitude north of the equator as Cape Town has south.

While in many places climate is determined by physical geographical features, across much of Africa climate conforms to a general symmetrical pattern which radiates out from the equator. Moving north and south from year-round rain in the Congo Basin, regions receive less and less rain over fewer months until at the Sahara Desert in the north, and the Namib and Kalahari deserts in the south, rainfall is negligible.

The deserts are roughly centred around the Tropic of Cancer (Sahara) and the Tropic of Capricorn (Namib and Kalahari) which are 23.5 degrees north and south of the equator, marking the furthest point from the equator that the sun reaches directly overhead. At these limits this only happens on the solstices (21 June and 21 December). Further north and south of the deserts, Morocco's Atlas Mountains and South Africa's Drakensberg range have climates cold enough to allow winter snow-skiing.

For a continent that is often thought of as hot, flat and dry, Africa has a diverse range of climates and geographical features, and in true African style, things are done on a grand scale. There are swamps larger than countries, volcanoes nearly 6 kilometres (4 miles) high (higher than any of Europe's mountains), a desert as large as some continents, as well as glaciers, vast rivers and massive lakes.

FLORA

Africa's enormous variety of plants have adapted to its diverse environments, from high altitude and sub-zero temperatures on some of the mountains, to years of drought and searing heat in Africa's deserts.

But it is the very wet, hot and humid rainforest of the Congo Basin that supports more plant species than any other environment. A few hectares of rainforest holds more tree species than in the whole of Europe, and although only covering 7 percent of the earth's surface (previously 15 percent), rainforests contain over half of the world's plant species. The rainforests of Central and West Africa are multi-layered worlds of plants, mammals, insects, reptiles and birds. Arboreal highways link these layers together, enabling some animals to live in the forest canopy without ever touching the ground. It is the same for many plant species that grow in the cracks and crevices of the giant forest trees – up to 30 species may live on a single tree.

Many trees have large triangular, woody buttresses supporting their trunks from a generally shallow root system. Forest people like the Pygmies use the buttress as as 'drums' for dancing to, or as a bush telegraph – when hit, the buttresses give a deep, resonating sound that travels through thick vegetation.

Bamboo is another forest plant with a variety of uses, particularly in building. While bamboo may be the world's largest grass, it is on the savanna that grasses have come to dominate. The open plains typify big game country, and often it is the wildlife that plays a large part in keeping the savanna free of scrub and trees. Where trees do occur, they often embody an African trademark, the flat-topped acacia tree. Dozens of species of acacia occur, including the yellow fever tree and the whistling thorn, and in very arid areas the camel thorn is often found near dry riverbeds where its roots will grow down some 50 metres (165 feet) to reach water.

Also synonymous with Africa is the baobab tree. The baobab is special in many ways and is ingrained into African legends, often as a tree that was discarded by the gods and ended upside-down with its roots in the air – easy to understand considering the tree's unusually large girth and often bare branches. Virtually all of its parts can be used, from making food and medicines to glues, soaps and cloth fibres, although not on a highly commercial level.

Economically valuable for their timber are trees like mahogany, which is prized for furniture, and ebony, whose dark heartwood is very hard and can be highly polished to make items ranging from carved souvenirs to piano keys. The marula tree's small fruits are made into a liqueur – animals like baboons and elephants also eat the fruits and sometimes become drunk when the fruits ferment in their stomachs. Indigenous to Ethiopia is the coffee tree, now very important to the economies of many countries.

In other tree species it is the gum resins that have commercial value. The finest type of gum Arabic, used for a huge variety of purposes from medicine to artwork, comes from some species of acacia tree. The most important gum resin is probably latex from which rubber is made. Other main gum resins, particularly in the Horn of Africa, are the incenses of frankincense and myrrh, both of which will harden on contact with air.

Although not commercially significant, there are several highly unusual and unique plants in Southern Africa's Namib Desert. Among them is the welwitschia plant, which only ever bears two strap-like leaves in its lifetime (and which sometimes lives over 1 000 years). The leaves come from a short, stumpy protrusion on an immense underground tap-root, so the plant is well adapted to minimize moisture loss, and can store water over long, dry spells. The *kokerboom*, a relative of the aloe, is another unusual tree adapted to hot, dry conditions. Their spiky, succulent leaves, by having a small surface area, maximize moisture content while minimizing moisture loss.

Southern Africa also boasts some special floral kingdoms. Namaqualand in South Africa is probably the most famous in the region for its vivid and spectacular display of spring wild flowers. Many of the flowers have special mechanisms for germinating, enabling them to survive in this semi-arid area.

Indigenous to South Africa are over 8 000 species of the Cape Floral Kingdom. Only six floral kingdoms exist world-wide, with most of the others spread over several continents. Altogether it is estimated that South Africa alone contains 10 percent of the world's plant species. Much of the Cape Floral Kingdom consists of *fynbos* ('fine bush') species which include proteas, watsonias and ericas.

Elsewhere in Africa are 'islands' of plant species that have adapted to isolated microclimates. The constant spray from Victoria Falls has created a miniature rainforest in the middle of dry bushveld, a microclimate containing some plant species that cannot be found within 1 000 kilometres (621 miles).

In East Africa are unique Afro-alpine zones on the slopes of the equatorial mountains. Many species grow to several times their normal size, like giant lobelias and groundsels, some of which have special mechanisms to protect them from sub-zero night-time temperatures. This includes leaves protectively closing over their central bud at night, and retaining dead leaves and flowers as insulation.

The use of plants in traditional medicine is still widespread in Africa. For years Western medical experts ridiculed African 'witch

BELOW *These baobab trees in the Kalahari Desert, Botswana, look little different from when Thomas Baines painted them in 1862.*

doctors', but now plants that have been used by Africans for generations are being tested, with some startling results. The common sausage tree that has been used by traditional doctors to treat skin conditions, has been found to contain properties that kill skin cancer. A type of periwinkle from Madagascar has a high success rate in curing forms of leukaemia that were previously almost always fatal, and the world's first natural tranquillizer came from a medicine made by a Nigerian witch doctor. Derived from the rauwolfia root, the medicine also produced a popular drug for high blood pressure.

Many plants are economically important to Africa, and although often thought of as native to the continent, a large number, such as tobacco, pineapples, avocados, oranges, tea,

BELOW *A carpet of vivid wild flowers form an annual spring spectacle in South Africa's Namaqualand region.*
OPPOSITE *With its square, flat lip, the white rhino is well suited to grazing grass.*

cloves and maize, have been introduced. Indigenous species have adapted to isolated environments, and particularly to hostile environments. Like Africa's wildlife, plant species have found niches in virtually every region of this vast and varied land.

WILDLIFE

The name Africa is synonymous with wildlife, and it is the incredible variety, as well as individual species, that makes the continent unique. For many people the elephant is the symbol of African wildlife, for others it is the lion that evokes images of the vast unspoilt and untamed savanna, where all forms of wildlife roam freely in their natural state.

BIG GAME

Few animals have endeared themselves to human beings as much as the African elephant. The largest of all land mammals, elephant have adapted and evolved to dominate their habitat, and have no real enemies except for man, although this has

exceptions – depending on the situation, elephant may also have to evade rhinoceros, lion or hippopotamus.

In some places elephants have adapted substantially to their environment. Compared to an average African elephant which grows to 3 or 4 metres (10 or 13 feet) and weighs up to 5 tonne or more, the elephants of the Central Africa forests only grow to 2 or 3 metres tall [6.5 or 10 feet]), and have smaller ears and downward pointing tusks. In the deserts of northern Namibia elephants have adapted to going without water for three to four days, instead of drinking every day. To assist in the long distances they travel, they are generally taller with longer legs than most elephants.

Another large African wildlife icon is the rhinoceros. From the early 20th century when settlers described them as being as plentiful as cattle, white hunters came in and took their toll. What the hunters left have in recent years been decimated by African poachers who supply the horns to Arab dagger manufacturers and Asian medicine men.

One of Africa's animals whose population seems to be holding its own is the hippopotamus. This highly territorial and often aggressive vegetarian is responsible for more human deaths than any other large African mammal, mainly through drownings from capsized canoes. However, if they do decide to attack, their massive jaws and tusk-like canine teeth can cut a person (or a crocodile) in half.

As well as the biggest land mammal, Africa is also the home to the tallest one. The giraffe can grow up to 6 metres (20 feet), which enables it to browse on the succulent leaves at the tops of trees. While baby giraffe are vulnerable to attack, adults are usually a fairly even match against predators, being able to kick in virtually any direction – powerfully enough to break a lion's back.

A giraffe at a gallop – seen as a gentle rocking movement as if in slow motion – must be one of the most graceful sights on the African plains. This slow gracefulness is deceptive as the giraffe can move at up to 60 kilometres (37 miles) per hour.

PREDATORS

It is probably the lion that tourists on safari would hope to see more than any other animal, and to hear one roar in the wilds of Africa is a very special experience. One, two or sometimes three males (often brothers) will usually lead a pride of females and young for one to three years. When sub-adult males are between one and a half to three and a half years old, they are forced to leave the pride but, depending on their strength, they may eventually take over their own pride. When this happens, the new male usually kills all of the small cubs, so strong is his instinct to sow his own genes. Females with dead cubs will usually come into oestrus immediately instead of two years after the cubs' birth. If mating with

the new male is successful (they mate up to 100 times a day for several days), three and a half months later a new litter will be born.

While lions and virtually all predators will scavenge when they can, the cheetah will usually only eat what it has freshly killed itself – one of many habits that go against its general survival. But they face further, more serious problems. They have a very narrow gene pool and it is thought that this has contributed to up to 75 percent of males being infertile: of all the cheetah cubs that survive to be adults (and the mortality rate is high) only one in eight will be a fertile male. Add to this the fact that the female usually requires several males to compete for her before she will mate, and the chance of a fertile mating becomes slim.

The third of Africa's large cats, the leopard, is extremely strong and can take prey that weighs more than itself high into trees. In this way they protect their kill from other carnivores. While leopard seem to favour medium-sized antelope as prey, they will eat just about anything from

insects to rodents, birds, fish, reptiles, small mammals and even other carnivores (dogs and jackals). Leopards like to be close to a water source, but in very dry regions they get the moisture they need from their prey's blood and can go for long periods without drinking.

Seven species of small cat are found in Africa. With its long tufted ears the caracal is sometimes called the African lynx, its name originally deriving from the Turkish *karakal* meaning 'black ears'. About twice the height and length of a domestic cat, the caracal is adept at leaping and catching birds in flight. The serval, another small cat, can also leap high (3 metres; 10 feet) into the air to catch birds, but is not as expert as the caracal.

Cats traditionally kill with a neck or throat hold, but the hyena has a double advantage of a much stronger bite and big, powerful neck muscles, giving it a hierarchy above all cats except lions (and even lions are chased from a kill if hyenas sufficiently outnumber them). Research has found that hyenas, previously thought to be scavengers, are highly efficient hunters, but when it comes to scavenging, they are without rival. Hyenas are particularly curious and have an acute sense of smell. Vehicle tyres that may have driven through animal dung sometimes arouse their interest. With their powerful jaws they have been known to puncture tyres, eat hinges off camp fridges, and devour soap for its animal fat content – a good reason to leave toiletries, food and anything that smells, locked in a vehicle when camping in the bush.

Over the years the African wild dog has been persecuted by farmers, hunters, and even park officials who, due to ignorance, have all slaughtered them. Also known as the Cape hunting dog, wild dogs kill their prey by disembowelling – something that many people find inhumane if they apply human values to wild animals. The scientific name of the endangered wild dog is *Lycaon pictus* meaning 'painted wolf'. Each pack member can be identified by its individual markings of dark brown, black, white and yellow patches. The wild dog is often thought of as a domestic dog gone wild, but it is a separate species.

Many of the jackal's characteristics and habits are dog-like and it is possible that domestic dogs descended from a species of jackal. Jackals eat fruits and berries as well as anything small such as insects, rodents, snakes, birds and small antelope. They will take any carrion they can steal from a larger predator, and on Namibia's Skeleton Coast, jackals will eat seal pups and marine carrion.

Related to jackals and wild dogs are several species of fox. The sand fox, red fox, fennec, and Ruppell's fox all have ranges in and around the Sahara Desert, while the rare Simien fox is found only in Ethiopia. The bat-eared fox, like most foxes, is nocturnal, and uses its oversized ears like radar to detect insects and small mammals.

HERBIVORES

Buffalo, along with lion, elephant, rhino and leopard, have the rather dubious honour of being part of the 'Big Five' – the top five animals on a hunter's 'most wanted' list. Despite this, buffalo are still numerous, and form herds of up to 2 000 beasts. Of all the animals of the African plains, it is the buffalo that hunters are most wary of. The tale of a wounded buffalo doubling back to ambush a hunter is a familiar story.

Another herbivore common on the African plains is the zebra. They usually walk in single file, following a strict hierarchy. While one male is in charge of up to six females and any foals they may have, he will usually let the top ranking female lead them to fresh pasture, a

waterhole, or wherever she decides. Following the lead female are the other females in descending order of rank. However, foals take on the rank of their mother and are respected by lesser ranked adult females. Mares usually stay in one family group their whole lives.

In the Horn of Africa lives the endangered wild ass. Distantly related to zebras, the wild ass is virtually indistinguishable from domestic donkeys that have gone wild. Of the two types of wild ass – the Nubian and Somali – it is the Somali that can be distinguished by zebra-like bands of black and white across its lower legs.

Antelope are the largest group of herbivores on the plains, ranging from the minute 25-centimetre-tall (10 inch) royal antelope of West Africa to the massive eland, Africa's largest antelope. Despite weighing up to 1 000 kilograms (2 200 pounds), eland are very good at jumping and have been known to leap over other eland. Impala and many gazelle species are also known for their jumping, or 'pronking'. This behaviour of bounding, often in a zigzagging course, is sometimes seen when they are fleeing a predator. Although actually slowing them down, it shows the predator that the antelope is fit and healthy.

Many antelope have adapted to specific environments. Some, like the oryx (gemsbok), have adapted to near-desert conditions, while others, like the waterbuck and sitatunga, are happy in swamps and water (the sitatunga will almost completely submerge itself to avoid predators). The darkly coloured bongo is a nocturnal forest antelope and the tiny dikdik, so called because of its alarm call, prefers thick, dry bush and undergrowth.

Some of the more prominent members of the antelope family are the majestic kudu with its huge 'corkscrew' horns (on the male only), and the striking sable bull, almost jet-black in colour with long scimitar horns.

Arguably the most famous antelope is the clown of the African plains, the wildebeest. With its strange looks and crazy zigzagging running style, it has a place in many African myths as being made up of spare or leftover parts. The East African wildebeest, also known as the white bearded gnu, has in recent times attracted attention for its mass migration of up to 1.5 million animals between Tanzania's Serengeti plains and Kenya's Masai Mara National Reserve.

SMALL MAMMALS

A bewildering number of diverse species of small mammals have evolved in Africa, often sharing the same habitat as the plains grazers, although because of their size and habits (like being nocturnal), many are seldom seen.

Several species have developed unusual defence systems. The zorilla, or striped polecat, not only looks similar to the American skunk, but also has a nauseating chemical defence. Another small black and white mammal, the honey badger, or ratel, secretes a chemical from an anal gland that is said to stupefy bees, enabling the honey badger to raid bees' nests for honey. It is one of the most ferocious animals in Africa. When disturbed by large animals it will bite and rake at their underbelly with its strong legs and sharp claws, and has even been known to kill buffalo in this manner.

The civet has become famous for its scent glands as it secretes musk which is used in perfume (unfortunately to collect musk, civets are often kept in cages no bigger than themselves). Related to the civet is the mongoose, most species of which are solitary and nocturnal, and therefore seldom seen. Mongooses have a reputation for killing snakes, but only very occasionally do so, feeding mainly on insects and small mammals. Suricates and meerkats, along with other types of mongoose, have the habit of standing up on their rear legs to look around if they suspect danger – a habit that is shared by ground squirrels who also have the tendency to curl their big fluffy tails back over their heads as a sun umbrella.

Other small mammals have more unusual defence systems. The pangolin, or scaly anteater, has protective overlapping scales, and the porcupine is known for its long, sharp quills. Up to a metre (3 feet) long, porcupines do not always defend themselves by staying still, and if threatened can charge backwards – the direction in which their quills point.

Just as strange is the aardvark, a nocturnal and seldom seen mammal that uses its oversized snout and ears to find the termites and ants on which it almost exclusively feeds. With its name deriving from the Afrikaans for earth pig, the aardvark digs large, often maze-like burrows that provide housing for a variety of animals from hyenas to snakes. Of the African wild pigs, it is the warthog that is most commonly sighted. So called because of wart-like lumps on its head, it is often seen 'kneeling' on its front knees as it grazes, and running with its tail in the air – a characteristic that is thought to enable a family to follow each other when fleeing through long grass.

PRIMATES

Perhaps more than any other animals in Africa, humans identify most with primates, in particular the apes – chimpanzees and gorillas. Chimps are the closest living relatives to humans, sharing 98 percent of our genes.

RIGHT *The gemsbok can withstand extreme heat due to special nasal blood vessels which cool blood on the way to the brain.*

ABOVE *An interesting trait of crocodiles is that the sex of hatchlings is decided by the temperature at which the eggs are incubated.* OPPOSITE *The majestic bateleur eagle, seen here in Chobe National Park, Botswana.*

In groups that have been studied, individuals show distinct personalities and their similarities with humans have made them popular with medical researchers. With tens of thousands of dollars at stake, many baby chimpanzees are captured to be sold to laboratories and as exotic pets. As a consequence, it is usual for a whole family to be shot trying to defend the baby and, as many orphans die without their mothers, there can be dozens of deaths for each baby that lives.

While chimpanzees are killed and captured in the name of research, mountain gorillas face different threats. Their main problems are loss of habitat, getting caught in snares set for other animals, and frequent insecurity due to civil war in the small region in which they live. With no mountain gorillas held in a captive environment anywhere, and under 500 left in the wild, their situation is precarious.

Each family group of mountain gorillas is led by a dominant male, whose black coat has turned silver down his back. Young gorillas sometimes play in trees but adults are largely terrestrial and seldom venture off the ground. They do not like getting wet and during rains they will often sit miserable and still in a human-like posture, with head bowed and shoulders hunched. Each night they build new nests out of sticks, grass and leaves, usually on the ground and, although nomadic, they have a home range in which they stay.

A primate that is much more widespread than the gorilla is the baboon, which lives in troops of up to 200. Group members have a definite hierarchy or rank, and communicate with each other via a series of 30 or so gestures and over a dozen sounds. Babies are carried slung underneath their mother's belly, and when bigger will ride 'piggy back' on their mother's rump. Although reasonably good climbers, baboons tend to live on open ground, climbing trees to sleep, to avoid predators and sometimes to eat.

As well as the commonly seen baboons – the chacma in the south, yellow or common baboon in the east and the anubus or olive baboon from parts of East to West Africa – there are four very different looking baboons, each restricted to a relatively small range. The mandrill and drill both have bright blue and red on some of their bare parts, and are found in separate pockets of rainforest in Cameroon. Favouring as a habitat the high altitude clifftops in Ethiopia is the gelada, unmistakable with a long mane and a bright red bare patch on its chest. Nearby, with a range bordering on the Red Sea, is the ashy grey hamadryas which has a bright pink face and rump.

Of the dozens of species and subspecies of monkey in Africa, none is as common as the vervet. They are less arboreal than virtually all other monkeys, preferring instead open savannas, and have adapted to eat a large variety of plants and animals including flowers, bark, leaves and roots, insects, eggs and small mammals. It is probably this diversification and the large areas of suitable habitats that have led to their success in numbers and range.

Other monkeys of the guenon, mangaby and colobus families generally prefer forests. Some, like the red-eared nose-spotted monkey are confined to small remnants of West African rainforest, while others like the black-cheeked white-nosed monkey live throughout large tracts of Central African rainforests.

One of the smallest primates is the bush-baby, or galago. Nocturnal forest-dwelling creatures, they seldom come to ground, are timid and only occasionally seen, but are often heard. The bush-baby has several different calls, some of which resemble human screams and cries – an unnerving sound in a dark forest.

REPTILES

Humans seem to have an innate fear of reptiles, particularly crocodiles and snakes. Most feared of all snakes is the black mamba which is

known by some African peoples as the 'two step' (because they say that this is as far as you will get if you are bitten by one). The black mamba is supposedly more aggressive than other snakes but more often than not it will react as most snakes do if they encounter humans – slither off as quickly as possible. Other feared snakes are the puff adder (part of the viper family), which gets its name from its loud exhaling noise, the spitting cobra, which can squirt venom accurately at a victim's eyes, and the non-poisonous python, a constrictor which can grow to 6 metres (20 feet) long.

Reaching a similar length are Nile crocodiles, another reptile with a reputation that is feared, and deservedly so. Crocodiles are thought to recognize daily habits of victims, and have been known to wait in ambush not only at the water's edge, but also beside pathways through the bush.

Other reptiles include the Nile monitor lizard, which can grow up to 2 metres (6.5 feet) in length, and the chameleon, famous for changing colour. Entrenched into African

traditional legends and myths, the chameleon has several strange habits. Its coiled, sticky tongue can catch insects almost the length of the chameleon's body away, it has a strange, slow, rocking walk, and its eyes can move independently – being on the sides of its head, one can look back while the other looks forward. In some African legends this converts to being able to see into the past and future.

Although chameleon coloration often very closely resembles its environment, scientists believe its colour changes are not for specific camouflaging, but are due to mood changes. At least a hundred species of chameleon occur, including several with horns and one that grows up to nearly half a metre (1½ feet) long.

BIRDS

Africa has such a variety of bird species of all sizes and colours that uninterested visitors often return home avid bird-watchers. It is difficult not to be impressed by millions of pink flamingos, the majesty of a fish eagle dropping from the sky to snatch a fish, the pastel colours of the lilacbreasted roller, or a graceful heron in flight. The list of the strange and unusual, colourful and attractive, is exhaustive. Over 400 different species of bird in a single game park is not uncommon.

Most obvious on the African plains is the world's largest bird, the ostrich. Although it is flightless, the ostrich is capable of running at speeds of up to 70 kilometres per hour (44 miles per hour). The kori bustard is the world's heaviest flying bird, weighing up to 20 kilograms (44 pounds), although it is almost always seen on the ground. Sometimes brightly coloured carmine bee-eaters will use the big bird as a perch, catching insects that buzz around the kori bustard's head. Competing with the kori bustard as the world's largest flying bird, in wingspan rather than weight, is the marabou stork, with bigger birds having a wing span of over 3 metres (10 feet). The marabou is often seen scavenging rubbish, or waiting its turn behind vultures at a kill as, although larger than vultures, it has a different bill and is unable to rip meat from the bone.

Other members of the stork family are also impressive. The saddlebilled stork is a very tall, elegant black and white bird with a bright red and yellow 30-centimetre-long (12 inches) bill. The massive whale headed stork, or shoebill, is an almost prehistoric-looking bird with its boot-shaped and -sized bill.

Also with an unusual bill are the various species of hornbill. Females have the odd habit of sealing themselves inside their nests (usually in a hollow tree) while the males feed them and their chicks through a narrow slot.

With African jacanas, it is their feet rather than their bills that have adapted to suit a particular niche in the ecosystem. With extraordinarily long toes, their weight is spread out, enabling them to walk across lilies and floating aquatic vegetation, giving them the alternative name of lilytrotter.

Oxpeckers have also found a niche, using the mobile perches of giraffe, buffalo, zebra, rhino and the like as semi-permanent homes, even sleeping and mating there. Their symbiotic relationship provides them with insects while ridding their hosts of pests and keeping a lookout for predators. Some egrets have a similar relationship, particularly with buffalo; however, more often they will be close by on the ground foraging for insects that the buffalo disturbs.

Another symbiotic relationship exists between the honeyguide and the honey badger (or ratel). The honeyguide will lead the badger to beehives and share the spoils after the animal has ripped the hive open. They are known to lead humans in the same way.

Weaver birds also have an interesting habit. As their name suggests, they actually weave their nests and are capable of several different stitches and knots. It is the male bird that does the weaving, and his ability to attract a female depends on his nest-building ability, which she will check. Various weavers have different designs of nest, usually based around a ball shape and often with a long tubular entrance. Most spectacular of all are the sociable weavers who form colonies of hundreds in enormous communal nests.

Strange habits proliferate in the African bird world. In the mountains of Ethiopia and South Africa bones falling from the sky inevitably come from a lammergeier, or bearded vulture. The large birds are very accurate at hitting rocks (of which they have favourites) with the bones they drop, after which they will land to eat the splintered bone.

If the vultures are some of the ugliest large birds, then the crowned crane must be one of the most beautiful. Atop an elegant grey body and red, white and black head, sits a golden, bristling plume. Another lovely bird is the secretary bird. At over a metre (3 feet) tall with an orange-yellow face, this large white bird has particularly strong legs and feet and is usually seen walking through grassland in search of rodents and snakes. Its name is often said to come from its crest which is comprised of pen-like quills (placed behind the ear in the manner of an old-fashioned secretary), but it derives from its original Arabic name *saqr-et-tair*, which means 'hunter bird'.

Louries, or turacos, are also attractive birds dressed in bright greens, blues, purples, and often with a dash of red under the wings which is very conspicuous in flight. The plain grey lourie is also called the 'go away' bird because of its warning 'gorway' call when it senses danger, such as approaching humans.

Plovers also give a warning call which is a high-pitched 'pip pip pip'. They are also known to 'dive bomb' humans if they come too close to a clutch of eggs which are usually hidden on the ground. The African fish eagle has a haunting call that to many people is one of the most evocative sounds of wild Africa. But the best 'talker' of all is the African grey parrot and domestic birds are prized world-wide for their mimicry of the human voice. In parts of West Africa they can be seen in flocks of hundreds, identifiable by their very rapid wingbeat and blood-red colouring under their tail.

The diversity of African birdlife is too great to list here. Arguably even more so than the mammals, birds have adapted and evolved to Africa's wide range of habitats.

CONSERVATION

Despite a large number of African wildlife species, the list is not as long as it once was, nor do individual species occur in the same numbers. It is unlikely that Africa will ever again see the masses of wildlife that covered parts of South Africa in the 18th and 19th centuries, or East Africa in the early 20th century. Many animals have become extinct, particularly in the very north and very south of the continent, where man has come to dominate the environment more than anywhere else. Gone from North Africa is the Atlas bear and the Barbary lion. Another lion, the Cape lion, was killed off in its Southern African range. Southern Africa has also lost several other indigenous species including the zebra-like quagga, the Cape red hartebeest and the bluebuck. Perhaps the most famous extinction is the dodo bird from Mauritius.

In recent times other major species have come under threat. Most notably and most widely publicized has been the elephant,

killed by poachers for their ivory tusks. Until the 1989 Convention on International Trade in Endangered Species (CITES) ban on international trade in ivory, African elephants were being killed at up to 100 000 per year, leaving just 600 000. Since the agreement numbers have stabilized, but at the 1997 CITES conference, it was decided to allow limited trade in ivory in some countries. Although this may benefit these countries to some extent, it also puts the rest of Africa's elephants at risk.

Cheetah populations have also declined to numbers that make their extinction, at least from wild areas, a real possibility in the near future. Only one country, Namibia, has a reasonable population. But even Namibia's 2 000 or so cheetah should be compared to three times that number that were reported

shot (and the many more that were not reported) during the 1980s alone. The most endangered of Africa's large carnivores is the African wild dog. Now extinct in 19 out of 33 countries in which it once existed, its social nature has made it the victim of contagious diseases. The wild dog has also suffered from its undeserved reputation with many farmers shooting whole packs as vermin, whether the dogs have been bothering stock or not.

But there are also great success stories. The parks of East and Southern Africa have become very popular with tourists, earning their countries valuable foreign currency. When wildlife has a greater value alive than dead, it is better protected. Recently there have been moves to share that income with the people who live around the parks.

ABOVE *Graceful giraffe gallop across the plains of the Okavango Delta in Botswana.*

Essentially conservation is a first world ideal – something of concern only after people have the basic necessities like food, shelter and health care. For those Africans who do not have this security, feeding their family by whatever means possible is a far higher priority than saving wildlife.

Currently it is the visitors to game parks who are the saviours of wildlife. Without them, millions of years of evolution could be gone in a historical blink of an eye. All efforts to conserve wildlife must be kept up, or in a generation we could be talking of elephant and rhino in the same way we do of dinosaurs.

NORTH AFRICA

Acting as a natural barrier of some 5 000 kilometres (3 100 miles) and stretching from the Atlantic Ocean to the Red Sea, the Sahara Desert has effectively cut North Africa off from the rest of the continent. Despite centuries of trans-Saharan trade bringing riches of gold, ivory and slaves from the south, North Africa has closer ties to the Middle East and Europe than to the rest of Africa. It has developed its own cultures, influenced and at times dominated by regional civilizations including the Greeks, the Phoenicians, the Romans, the Arabs and the Europeans. While endeavouring to remain autonomous, the Berbers, the region's original inhabitants, have also made their presence felt.

Evidence still exists of the occupations of ancient civilizations who have left their ruined cities dotted along the North African coast, and even today societies from the past continue with their mediaeval lifestyles: step through the gates of one of Morocco's ancient walled cities and another time and place is revealed.

Once the capital of Morocco, Fez is sometimes described as the largest functioning mediaeval city in the world. It is also seen as a place of great spiritual and cultural learning, and its university dates back to around 860AD.

Some 400 000 people reside in Fez's old town, or Medina, leading lives little different from those who resided there a thousand years ago. A maze of narrow, crooked alleys is squeezed in by thousands of buildings, leaving no room for modern transport. Through doorways comes the tapping sounds of silversmiths hammering out patterns on silver, brass and copper plates, while the lower, dull, thudding noises of the leather workers can be heard through open shuttered windows and doorways. Piles of brightly

PREVIOUS PAGES *A traditional street vendor dispenses spring water in Marrakech.*
OPPOSITE *Elaborate tile mosaics decorate the Karouine Mosque in Fez, Morocco.*
BELOW *The kasbah (citadel) in Rabat, Morocco, overlooks the Bou Regreg River.*

coloured olives, decorated with fresh fruits and chillies, are displayed beside pyramids of exotic spices, all dappled by sunlight filtering through overhead latticework sunscreens. The heady scent of sandalwood and incense burning on charcoal fires mix with the aromas of spices and fruit.

It is easy to become disorientated and completely lost – a very real and potentially serious problem in Fez Medina. Tourists have been known to be lost for days in the labyrinth of alleys. Constantly busy with the traffic of people and donkeys, some alleys are also lined with market stalls, forming noisy bazaars. However, it is also possible to turn a corner and find it suddenly still and eerily silent with nobody around.

In the Medina certain areas, or souks, specialize in leatherware, carpets, metalwork or other products. Most visitors to Fez find themselves in a carpet shop at some stage. In a den of lavish hand-knotted wool or silk carpets, deals are discussed over traditional sweet mint tea. Moroccan salesmen are among the best in the business and pressure to buy can become enormous. Wool for carpets and blankets is hand-dyed and woven into geometric patterns (no animals or people may be depicted, as Islam forbids imitating Allah's creatures). Leather is also dyed traditionally in the famous Fez dye pits. Young apprentices stand waist-deep in the dye turning the hides, their legs becoming permanently discoloured.

While the ancient buildings of Europe live on in a context of modern structures and lifestyles, somehow depriving them of their age and history, Fez Medina epitomizes ancient history, alive today not only in its architecture, but also in its traditions. Here there are few reminders of the present century and the only form of transport is still the donkey. 'Balek, Balek!' is a common warning

shout in Fez Medina as donkey drivers yell to pedestrians to make way for their overloaded beasts of burden.

Just 60 kilometres (37.5 miles) away is the city of Meknes, which, like Fez, was once an ancient capital of Morocco. Founded by Berbers 1 000 years ago, Meknes became an imperial capital in the 17th century. Today it services the surrounding fertile countryside where olives, citrus fruit, grapes and cereals are grown. Massive walls with huge keyhole-shaped archways surround most of the old city which, though similar to Fez, is much smaller and less frenzied.

Rabat joins Meknes and Fez as one of Morocco's ancient imperial capitals but is also the current capital. This coastal city takes its name from a fortified monastery, or *ribat*, which was built in the 10th century at the mouth of the Bou Regreg River. Two centuries later a kasbah, or citadel, was built on the site of the old monastery and today still dominates the river. Across the river from the citadel lies the city of Salé – now really a suburb of Rabat. Both cities were prominent in the 1600s when their main revenue came from piracy.

About 200 kilometres (125 miles) south of Rabat, at the foot of the Atlas Mountains, lies Marrakech, yet another past imperial capital of Morocco, that for years has been a magnet for hippies and travellers. The name Morocco derives from Marrakech which in turn means 'fortified'. The city, along with Fez, was a major crossroads on the trans-Sahara trade routes, much in the same way that Morocco as a country is a melting pot of indigenous Berbers, Europeans, Africans and Arabs.

Within Marrakech's 800-year-old walls lies Place Djemaa el Fna, a large open square that comes alive at night when snake charmers, acrobats, storytellers, magicians, jugglers and fire-eaters emerge to perform among the food

stalls. Cafés and rooftop restaurants surround the square, and the bazaars and souks each offer their specialized crafts. Veiled Muslim women and men wearing jellabas – pointed hooded gowns – lend an air of mystery to the souks. The magic of Place Djemaa el Fna lures tourists and locals back night after night.

Overlooking Marrakech and stretching all the way to Tunisia is the 2 000-kilometre-long (1 200 miles) Atlas Mountain range, with the highest point, Mount Toubkal (4 165 metres; 13 674 feet) and the Oukaïmeden ski-field, not far from Marrakech. Named after the legendary Greek figure Atlas who held the world on his shoulders, the snowy peaks of the Atlas Mountains stand in stark contrast to the Sahara Desert which pushes its way right up to the mountain's southern slopes.

It is here, in this barren, dry, southern region of Morocco, that palm-fringed oases appear suddenly out of a shimmering heat haze – they are not mirages though. At the foot of the Atlas, Ait Benhaddou with its towering mud kasbah looks deceptively like an imposing city, but in reality is only a small village with a handful of residents. Film makers have rebuilt the village with large mud buildings for use in films such as *Lawrence of Arabia*, *Jesus of Nazareth* and *Jewel of the Nile*.

Further along the foot of the Atlas, a valley dotted with mud brick villages and palmeries gradually becomes deeper and narrower until it hits a massive rock wall. Todra Gorge, a spectacular fissure, in parts not much wider than its single lane road, tunnels its way deeply into the rock wall. Vertical sides tower 300 metres (1 000 feet) above the floor of the

OPPOSITE *Much of Morocco's famed leatherwork is tanned by tradesmen using traditional methods at the Fez dye pits.*

gorge, which in places is narrower at the top than at the bottom. The clear stream that runs down Todra Gorge – like most waterways that flow off the southern slopes of the Atlas – heads into the Sahara, then peters out.

In some way or another, the Sahara Desert dominates most of North Africa. This is particularly evident in Morocco's neighbour, Algeria, where 80 percent of Africa's second-biggest country is covered by the Sahara. A populated belt exists along the Mediterranean Sea but inland Algeria is sparsely inhabited, with only a handful of oasis towns. Sahara translates literally into the plural 'deserts' (of the singular *sahra*). This massive desert forms the largest dry area on the planet – an area almost the size of the United States or Europe.

Only a relatively small part – less than 20 percent – of the Sahara consists of sand dunes. The rest is made up of endless plains of sand or gravel, desolate stony plateaus and rocky mountains. In this landscape, combined with one of the world's hottest, driest climates, few animals or plants survive. The Sahara is even more inhospitable and unforgiving to humans. In the summer, without water or shade, life expectancy is less than a day. But the visitor to the Sahara will discover a beauty difficult to find elsewhere.

After driving for hours through a barren countryside, date palms surrounding small, mud-red towns seem like mirages. One such town, Taghit, sits at the foot of an enormous wall of sand that is the start of the Grand Erg Occidental (Great Western Sand Sea). Wave after wave of yellow sand, looking very much like a restless yellow ocean, carries on for over 400 kilometres (250 miles). At approximately 78 000 square kilometres (30 100 square miles) the Grand Erg Occidental is bigger than some countries (Ireland, for example) but still makes up less than one percent of the Sahara. Other

LEFT *Algeria's Grand Erg Occidental, or Great Western Sand Sea, stretches for hundreds of kilometres across the Sahara.* ABOVE *A Tuareg nomad's* tagilmust *(head-cloth) indicates the wearer's clan and status.*

ergs, such as the Grand Erg Oriental (Great Eastern Sand Sea), are larger still, while Issaouane-N-Tifernine has the world's highest dunes at 430 metres (1 411 feet).

At various sites around the desert, rock engravings and paintings, some dating back as far as 6000BC, show a different Sahara; one of green pastures and savanna where elephant, giraffe and gazelle roamed, much as they still do on the East African plains. Back then there were rivers with crocodiles, fish and hippo, and forests of cypress and oak. In some places it is possible to see glimpses of the past, such

as remnants of a petrified forest near In Salah in Algeria. By about 2500BC, the same time that the pyramids in Egypt were being built, the Sahara had started to become much drier. At this stage Saharan rock art indicates the presence of herds of cattle. Around 1200BC, artwork depicts horses and chariots and later still, as the desert became even drier, camels are shown. Over 30 000 examples of rock etchings and paintings can be found throughout the Sahara, with sites in all its mountainous regions, including the Ahaggar, or Hoggar Mountains. The Tassili region east of the Hoggars contains over half of the Sahara's known rock etchings and paintings.

The Hoggars cover a massive half million square kilometres (193 060 square miles) and are 2 916 metres (9 567 feet) at their highest point. On the western side of the Hoggars, a series of spectacular towering rock pinnacles transform the area into a lunar landscape. Once the pinnacles were all volcanoes, but erosion has worn away the outside, leaving just the inner cores, or volcanic plugs.

Over much of the Sahara, sub-zero night-time temperatures are common in the winter, but the weather high in the Hoggars is even more volatile with incredible winds and vast temperature differentials. At sunset, as the temperature plummets, cooling rocks make sharp cracking noises like fireworks. As the day ends and the curtain of darkness falls on the rock pinnacles, a new show begins. Perhaps because of the altitude and the clear, dry air over the Sahara, the night sky seems to be

PREVIOUS PAGES *Despite lying on the outskirts of Egypt's capital Cairo, the Great Pyramids of Giza retain a timeless majesty.*
RIGHT *Traditional feluccas sail on the Nile River at Aswan in Egypt.*

ablaze with starlight, and when the moon is full, its craters are clearly visible to the human eye and it casts a luminous glow on the sand.

At times the Saharan air is violently disrupted by sandstorms which can last several days and even weeks – potentially life-threatening for travellers. Annual seasonal winds occur from December to February when sand and dust blows off the Sahara and covers much of West Africa in a dusty haze for up to a quarter of the year.

The Sahara Desert also stretches into the historically interesting countries east of Algeria – Tunisia and Libya. Carthage, on the outskirts of Tunisia's capital Tunis, was once one of the most powerful cities in the world, rivalling Rome. It was founded by Phoenicians in 814BC who came from modern-day Lebanon and Syria. The most famous son of Carthage was Hannibal, who stormed across the Alps with his elephants to attack the Romans. At first he had considerable success against large numbers of Romans, but his power soon dwindled. After Hannibal's death (by suicide), the Romans laid siege to Carthage for three years, and finally destroyed it in 146BC.

However, a century later in 44BC (the year of Caesar's death), the Romans rebuilt Carthage and it became the capital of the Roman province of 'Africa'. The province grew until eventually the name became synonymous with the whole continent. It is thought that the name 'Africa' was initially the name of a local group of Berber cave dwellers. Today a modern suburb surrounds Carthage, with most of the remaining ruins dating from the Roman period.

Libya also boasts some significant ruins. Like Carthage, Leptus Magna was initially a Phoenician city and it too was taken by the Romans. But while Carthage was destroyed, Leptus Magna was left intact and became a major trading outpost. Many people believe

Leptus Magna, with its well-preserved arches, temples, forums, baths and walls, is the best example of Roman ruins in the Mediterranean.

Without a doubt Africa's finest ancient monuments are the pyramids in Egypt – not only the oldest but also the only fully surviving member of the 'Seven Wonders of the Ancient World'. More than 80 pyramids can be found in Egypt, but the Pyramid of Cheops at Giza on the outskirts of Cairo is the biggest – it is, in fact, the world's largest stone monument. It was built from around 2.3 million blocks of stone, each weighing an average of 2.5 tonnes, and reaches a height equivalent to a 40-storey building. Some of the stone used to erect this pyramid was quarried around Aswan High Dam before being transported more than 900 kilometres (560 miles) down the Nile to Giza.

Built over 4 500 years ago, the Pyramids of Giza were preceded by the first pyramid to be constructed, the 62-metre-high (203 feet) pyramid of Djoser, erected around 2650BC at Saqqara, Memphis, near Cairo. Two millennia after the Great Pyramids of Giza were built the Greek historian Herodotus called Egypt 'the gift of the Nile', because virtually all life in Egypt is sustained by the Nile – a quote that holds true even today, 2 500 years later.

The narrow, green strip of land that borders the Nile (just three percent of Egypt) supports 98 percent of the country's population. While people have lived on the banks of the Nile for millennia, it is only relatively recently that its source was discovered. In the second century AD, a Greek geographer, Ptolemy, guessed that the source of the Nile was two great lakes that received their water from the 'Mountains of the Moon', or Ruwenzoris. Without leaving Alexandria he had predicted what was only fully realized 17 centuries later. The Blue Nile rises from Lake Tana in the Ethiopian Highlands and the White Nile from the vast

Lake Victoria, shared by Tanzania, Kenya and Uganda. Many other sources also feed these lakes and the river, among them the Ruwenzori Mountains. The furthest source of the Nile was not discovered until 1937. From a small spring in Burundi, the Nile begins its 6 670-kilometre-long (4 145 mile) journey to the Mediterranean Sea.

Along the Nile in Egypt several other noteworthy historical sites can be found. Near the border of Sudan at Abu Simbel, two major temples were moved to higher ground in the 1960s to avoid flooding by the Aswan High Dam. These temples – of Ramses II and his wife Queen Nefertari – had been carved deep into cliffs at the edge of the Nile, and a massive 400 000 tonnes of temple had to be cut into pieces and erected at a higher level.

Built around 1300BC, these magnificent shrines were buried in sand and lost to the world until they were rediscovered in 1813. Perhaps because of their remote location, it was not until they were threatened with flooding that their true majesty became known world-wide. Sponsored by the United Nations Educational, Scientific and Cultural Organization (UNESCO), the salvage operation also took on another 30 or so smaller temples and monuments that would otherwise have been lost under the rising waters of the Aswan High Dam.

Approximately 200 kilometres (125 miles) north of Aswan lies Luxor (meaning 'place of palaces'), the Egyptian Empire's capital for nearly five centuries – from 1567BC to 1085BC. It is believed that Luxor has a higher concentration of ancient monuments and tombs than anywhere else in the world. The

OPPOSITE *An Aladdin's cave of intricately patterned brass, copper and silverware can be found in Cairo's bazaars.*

Luxor Temple, Karnak Temple Complex and Queen Hatshepsut's Temple are just three of the more outstanding examples.

It was in Luxor, in the Valley of Kings where over 30 royal tombs are sited, that the Tomb of Tutankhamen was unearthed in 1922. He was only 16 or 17 years old when he died, but what made his tomb stand apart from 61 others was that it had not been robbed of its treasures. It was discovered by archaeologist Howard Carter who, after digging unsuccessfully for six years, was about to have his funding ended when his search bore fruit. It took 10 years to remove and document the 1 700 treasures, which included a gold effigy of Tutankhamen, a solid gold coffin and two golden chariots.

Some 700 kilometres (440 miles) downstream from Luxor, Egypt's modern capital Cairo has asserted its dominance in the region. At the crossroads of Africa, Asia and Europe, its strategic position has been instrumental in it becoming the largest city in Africa, and bigger than any in the Middle East (to which it is perhaps more closely allied). Sitting astride the Nile, Cairo is a melting pot of East and West, old and new, Muslim and Christian. Minarets compete for space with modern apartment blocks, and cars choke the roads while people and markets fill the maze of narrow streets that form continuous bazaars. Museums hold the treasures of ancient dynasties while other monuments nearby remain *in situ*.

Cairo, like the whole of North Africa, remains culturally distinct from the rest of the continent. Even with modern technology and transport, the Sahara continues to separate and preserve the North as a unique region of Africa.

LEFT *Africa's largest city, Cairo, is a fascinating blend of old and new, and is a crossroads of people, religions and culture.*

ABOVE *Morocco, and particularly Marrakech, is known for its traditional entertainers.*
Story-tellers, acrobats, musicians and snake charmers are among those who continue to
perform their time-honoured crafts and professions.

OPPOSITE *An old route leads north from the Sahara Desert and through Morocco's*
spectacular Todra Gorge, a 300-metre-deep (1 000 feet) canyon. From here a rough track
heads high up into the Atlas Mountains via remote villages.

FOLLOWING PAGES *At the southern foot of the Atlas Mountains lie the impressive*
kasbahs (citadels) of Morocco's Ait Benhaddou. The town has guarded the pass over
the mountains to Marrakech for centuries, although today a new road has left Ait
Benhaddou a desolate place.

ABOVE *Although Berber nomads make up a very small part of Egypt's population, the arid environment away from the Nile River encourages a nomadic lifestyle.*

OPPOSITE *The interior of Mohammed Ali Mosque, Cairo, Egypt. The mosque, which took over 30 years to build (1824-1857), forms part of the Cairo Citadel and is a major landmark on the city's skyline.*

FOLLOWING PAGES *Ancient volcanoes have been eroded to leave only their inner cores in Algeria's Hoggar Mountains.*

ABOVE *The colossal figure of Ramses II, which sits outside the Great Temple at Abu Simbel in southern Egypt. Ramses II was one of ancient Egypt's most prolific builders and ruled for 67 years (1290-1224BC).*
RIGHT *At a distance, the smooth-looking sides of the Great Pyramids of Giza are deceptive. The Pyramids have large steps more than a metre (3 feet) high, and an overall height equivalent to a 40-storey office block.*
FOLLOWING PAGES *Egyptian architecture on the Red Sea coast at Hurghada – a town known as an excellent diving resort.*

NORTH AFRICA

LEFT *The underwater world of the Red Sea boasts abundant marine life, much of it unique. Many of its species have evolved in isolation as the Red Sea is virtually cut off from the open ocean.*
BELOW *The Great Rift has caused many of Africa's major geological features, including the Red Sea. Here, at the meeting point of Africa and Asia, the enormous variety of life found in the Rift Valley continues underwater.*
FOLLOWING PAGES *A typical street scene in Cairo, Egypt, where modern and traditional lifestyles exist side by side.*

WEST AFRICA

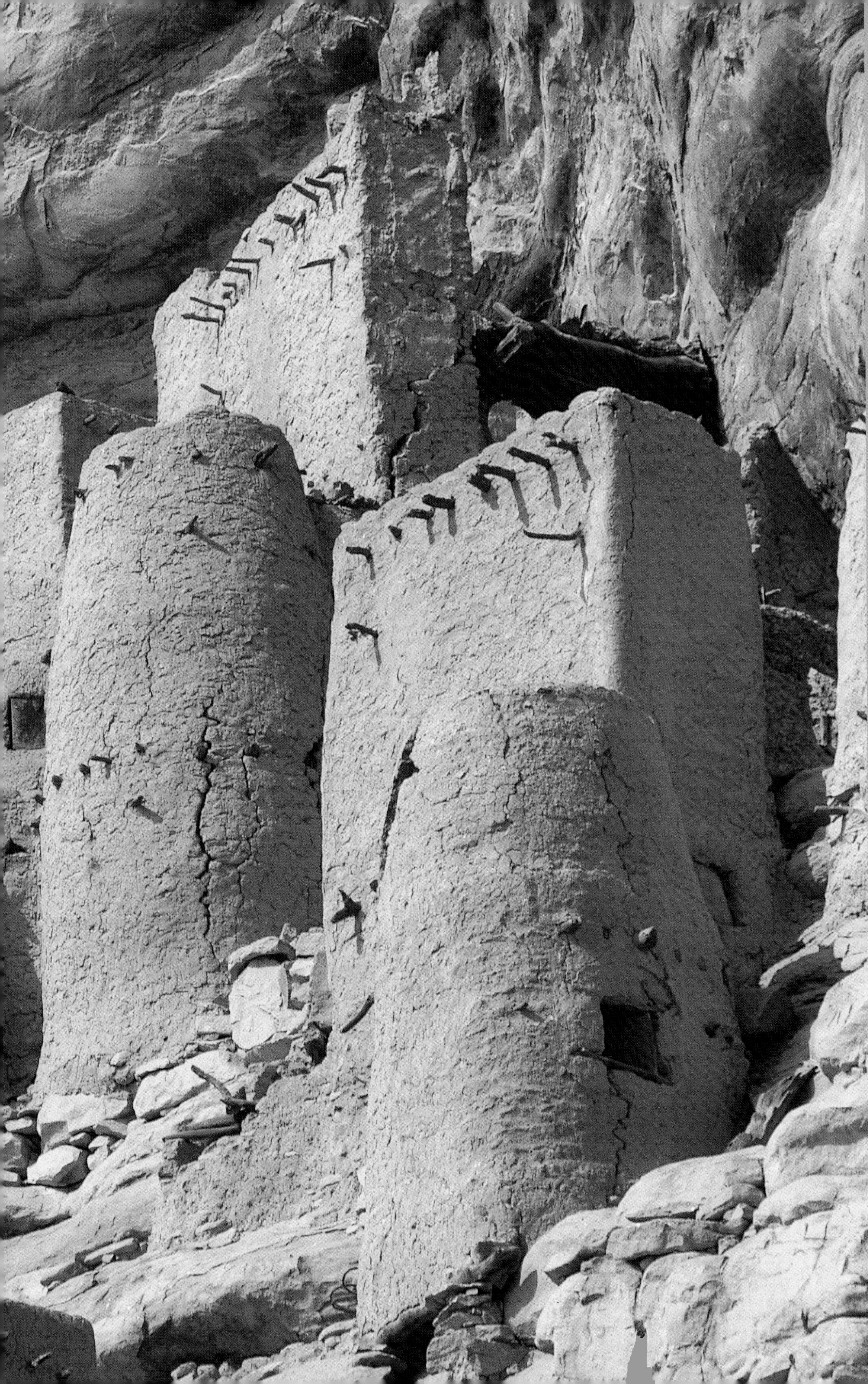

West Africa is a region where myths and legends merge with reality and tradition. Thousand-strong camel caravans led by Tuareg nomads still cross the Sahara Desert with their cargo of salt, and the fabled desert city of Timbuktu lives on. Even today, emirs, sultans and kings rule over kingdoms in several countries, and in many, voodoo and sacrifices continue to be practised. In small dusty villages in the Sahel, Peul women are still wearing pure gold earrings bigger than saucers. Some peoples who fled warring enemies centuries ago remain in their sanctuaries – the Dogon in the Bandiagara Cliffs, Mali, and the Tofinu people in a stilt village in Lake Nokoué, Benin.

In northern Cameroon dozens of skyscraper-sized rock pinnacles stretch skyward from the farmland. Known as Roumsiki's volcanic plugs, these spectacular pinnacles lie at the northern end of a volcanic mountain chain – the Mandara Mountains – that forms a natural border with Nigeria. Mount Cameroon is the tallest of the chain and is slightly separated from the main massif. Situated near the coast, this 4 070-metre-high (13 353 feet) active volcano is West Africa's tallest mountain.

Cameroon, although bordering Central Africa, is in many ways a microcosm of West Africa with its diversity in climate, people, vegetation, landscape and even colonial history. Because of its location, it has ethnic, linguistic and geographical ties to Central Africa. The northern parts are Muslim, while the south is Christian, although around 40 percent of Cameroonians still follow animistic beliefs. The official languages are French and English, but 160 African languages and dialects are also spoken. Cameroon was originally named by the Portuguese in 1472 after they mistook seasonal crayfish, found in an estuary near what is now Douala, for prawns (*cameroes*). In 1884 Germany set up the protectorate of 'Kamerun', but after Germany's defeat in World War I, the French and the British colonial powers came to control separate parts of Cameroon (hence the old plural term 'the Cameroons') from 1919.

In the north of Cameroon, near Roumsiki's volcanic plugs, live the Kirdi people. Their clusters of small, round huts and granaries with conical, millet-stalk roofs resemble groups of giant sharpened pencils on the steep hillsides. Like many tribes across West Africa, they still abide by their traditional animistic beliefs, many women piercing their lips, noses and ears and inserting pins and discs to ward off evil spirits. Kirdi, meaning 'infidel', was a name given to them by Cameroon's Muslim Fulanis, from whom they fled into the mountains.

In the northernmost parts of Cameroon, Waza National Park's 170 000 hectares (420 000 acres) of savanna grassland and forest

supports giraffe, lion, elephant and antelope, as well as prolific birdlife. From Waza, where it is dry nine months a year, to the Cameroon coast where Mount Cameroon is situated, the difference in climate could hardly be more extreme: the area around the mountain is one of the wettest in the world. Near to Mount Cameroon, on the border with Nigeria, lies Korup National Park, set up with the assistance of World Wide Fund for Nature (WWF). Korup consists of dense rainforest and here several species of monkey occur, as well as western lowland gorilla, chimpanzee and drill (a type of baboon found only in the Korup region).

One of Cameroon's most fascinating towns is Foumban where the fiercely independent Bamoun people have been ruled by a continuous line of sultans since the 1300s. This is one of the oldest direct descendent monarchies in the world. The 16th Sultan was noted for forming his own religion, language and script, and for building a European-styled palace during World War I.

In neighbouring Nigeria the oil boom of the 1960s and 1970s led to large-scale industrialization of its major cities, and thus overcrowding, traffic jams and pollution have become problems in many of them. Nigeria's population doubles every 19 years, but at present numbers over 100 million, making up around half of West Africa's population.

PREVIOUS PAGES *Mali's Dogon people cling precariously to an ancient way of life along the Bandiagara Escarpment.*
LEFT *Vibrantly coloured waxed cotton cloth is standard dress for women and girls across West Africa.*
OPPOSITE *A suspension footbridge marks the entrance to the primeval rainforest in Cameroon's Korup National Park.*

However, some northern cities retain the charm and character of a bygone era. A thousand years ago Kano was an important city on the trans-Saharan trade routes, and its old walled city still plays a very active part in Kano today. Craftsmen continue to ply their skills in time-honoured fashion: gold, silver and bronze are crafted by hand, cloth is woven and dyed in indigo and other natural dyes, and stalls line the busy, narrow alleys, reflecting little evidence of the present century. Within the walled city the Emir's Palace, built 500 years ago, is still being used by the current Emir.

Also prominent on the ancient Saharan trade routes are the northern cities of Katsina and Sokoto, dating back as far as the 11th and 12th centuries, and currently ruled by an emir and a sultan respectively. These cities are known for their festivals, particularly at the end of the Muslim fasting month of Ramadan, when their elaborately dressed leaders take part in processions along with cavalry in full regalia.

Near the centre of Nigeria lies Yankari Game Reserve where elephant are common. One of Yankari's main attractions is Wikki Warm Springs – a large spring suitable for swimming, with water so clear and pure that a pipe deep in its source collects the water to be bottled and sold as mineral water.

In Nigeria's southeast is Oshogbo, one of the continent's most important centres for African art. Highly regarded batiks, paintings, carvings and sculptures are produced by a network of artisans, some of whom are internationally renowned. On the outskirts of town the Sacred Forest is the home of various shrines to some of

the hundreds of Yoruba gods. The forest's surreal, eerie feeling, almost as if it were a living entity, is exaggerated by the sculpted, flowing forms of the shrines.

In the neighbouring countries of Benin and Togo, around 70 percent of the population follow animistic or traditional religions. These countries are known as the fetish and voodoo capitals of the world. Just outside Togo's capital Lomé lies Akodesséwa market, devoted to traditional medicines, fetishes and charms.

In Benin, according to the traditional beliefs of both the Tofinu and Fon people, fighting is not allowed in, on or near water because of a much revered water god. This caused the Tofinu to flee from the Fon in the 18th century and set up a stilt village in the middle of Lake Nokoué, where 10 000 people still live.

It is from the Fon people that we get the word voodoo, which literally means 'spirit'. Because of the slave trade from Africa, voodoo was taken to the Americas, particularly to the Carribean. Slaves were often separated from their friends and families and so hung on to the only thing they could – their traditional beliefs.

More than anywhere else in Africa the coast of Ghana pays testimony to the horrific export of humans from Africa. Seventy-six castles and forts that were used for holding slaves until ships arrived to transport them to the Americas once dotted the Ghanaian coastline. Many still exist. St George's Castle in Elmina, built by the Portuguese in 1482, is the oldest European building south of the Sahara Desert. Cape Coast Castle, another example, once held more than 1 000 slaves in ghastly conditions. Built in 1653 by the Swedes, it was run by the Danes, the local African ruler or *dey*, the Dutch and the English at various times. The French and the Germans also ran forts along Ghana's coastline. Slaves were often the victims of ethnic wars (where the main objective was usually to

collect slaves) and were then sold by African chiefs to the slave traders. Despite a centuries-long presence on the coast, Europeans seldom ventured inland because of these slave wars – many who did died due to disease or hostility from inland people, and thus the interior became known as 'The White Man's Grave'.

Ghana was and still is known for its large gold deposits, hence its former name of Gold Coast. After independence in 1957 (the first sub-Saharan nation to gain it), the country changed its name to Ghana, after the powerful 12th-century empire of Ghana that ruled much of West Africa (but not present-day Ghana).

Neighbouring Ghana is the Ivory Coast, officially Côte d'Ivoire. Because it had a lack of suitable harbours, the Ivory Coast had a lesser involvement in the slave trade. Today much of the idyllic coast is fringed with coconut palms, cocoa, banana and pineapple plantations – all plants introduced from Asia, the Americas and the Pacific.

Inland, in the west near the Ivory Coast's border with Liberia, live the Dan people. They too fled to escape warring factions, and settled in a forested, mountainous region. The Dan have become well-known for their artistic talents, particularly in mask-making and stilt-dancing. Stilt-dancers may spend several years learning their skills in a secret society, and when dancing, are considered to be part of the spirit world. The Dan people's homeland stretches across the border into Liberia. The national boundaries imposed by colonial powers ignored ethnic boundaries or geological features in a frantic effort by the Europeans to amass as much land as possible in the 'Scramble for Africa'.

Togo and Benin are typical examples of this with coastlines of only around 100 kilometres (60 miles) long each, but with inland borders stretching far into the interior. Liberia is the

OPPOSITE *With areas of the country receiving high rainfall, Cameroon has numerous impressive waterfalls such as this one on the border with Nigeria.*

only country on the African continent that was never colonized, or at least not by a European power. Freed American slaves established Liberia and despite making up only three percent of the population, dominated the indigenous people in politics and the economy until 1980. Since then civil unrest has prevailed in Liberia.

Under British control, neighbouring Sierra Leone (meaning 'lion mountain') also became a home for freed slaves, hence its capital's name of Freetown. Many slaves had come from ships – on their way to the Americas – that had been intercepted by the British Navy on anti-slaving patrols. The freed slaves were called Krios, or Creoles, and as in Liberia, they became the ruling elite despite comprising only two percent of the population. However, after independence in 1961, their power diminished considerably.

Further west are the coastal countries of Guinea and Guinea Bissau (Guinea is thought to have derived from the Berber word *aguinau* meaning 'black' [skinned people]). Guinea Bissau is one of the smallest countries in West Africa with a coastline indented with rivers and mangrove swamps, and dozens of offshore islands. A coin made of gold from the region derived its name from these two countries.

On the far west coast of Africa lies Senegal which totally surrounds (and is 17 times bigger than) the Gambia. One of the Gambia's claims to fame is that it is home to the village of Juffure, made famous in Alex Haley's book *Roots*. In Senegal the Island of Goree also played a major role in the slave trade, while just 3 kilometres (2 miles) away, the country's capital Dakar is well-known as the finishing point for the Paris-Dakar Motor Rally.

Between these coastal countries and the Sahara desert are three landlocked countries (Mali, Niger and Burkina Faso) dominated by the Sahel, a semi-arid region on the southern edge of the Sahara. Mali takes its name from an ancient empire that covered a much greater area than current-day Mali. The country's capital Bamako, situated on the banks of the great Niger River, is new by Malian standards: it is barely a century old. Despite this its Grand Marché, or large market, retains an old-world charm. Built in the Sudanic mud architecture style, a great castellated wall surrounds the bustling market. Inside, silver hand-crafted jewellery, ancient glass and ceramic trading beads, leather boxes, Tuareg swords and daggers, and wood carvings are all laid out on hand-woven textiles. The bright primary colours of women's wrap-around dresses and a feeling of vibrancy are typical of this and other West African markets.

The Sudanic mud architecture of Bamako's Grand Marché is also reflected further along the Niger River at Mali's Djenné. Entering Djenné is like entering a fairy tale. At the end of a long causeway the 1 000-year-old town sits on a flood plain island. After passing under a large, mud archway guarding the entrance to the town, a narrow dirt track twists its way between red mud buildings. Squeezing past dogs, donkeys, chickens, camels and people, the track winds past the encroaching walls to emerge onto a busy central market place.

Overshadowing the market is a large mud mosque. Internal timber framework pierces the outside of the building in a regular pattern, providing a permanent external scaffolding. Although this style of architecture is called Sudanic, it has little to do with the country of

RIGHT *After fleeing from warring tribes, the Tofinu people settled in Ganvie stilt village in the middle of Benin's Lake Nokoué and have now lived there for over two centuries.*

Sudan. Sudan translates loosely from the Arabic for 'black men'; the word previously applied to the whole Sahel region where Arabs first encountered black Africans.

As Djenné lies off both the Niger River, a main transport route, and the main road between Gão and Bamako, it has suffered economically and has been surpassed by the towns of Mopti, near the confluence of the Bani and Niger rivers, and Segou upstream on the Niger. Just 3 kilometres (2 miles) from Djenné, on another flood plain island, lies Jenné Jeno, the oldest-known city in West Africa. The city dates back as far as 250BC and archaeological finds show an African civilization that finally died out around 1400AD. Jenné Jeno was perhaps eclipsed by Djenné itself, which along with Timbuktu, had its peak around this time.

Timbuktu has been in decline for several centuries. In Europe it was originally known as a legendary place of vast riches – a great city of gold and learned men in the heart of the desert. As it turned out the legend was actually true, but for centuries no Europeans survived the journey to the city and back to Europe. Eventually a young Frenchman René Caillié, after learning Arabic, studying the Koran and disguising himself as a Muslim, reached Timbuktu in 1828, over a year after setting off from Senegal. By this time it was around four centuries after the legends had started and Timbuktu was more as it is today – a dusty, mud-brick town surrounded by desert. Naval exploration and trade had changed the course

LEFT *To villagers near Touba, Ivory Coast, the stilt dancer is a spirit, not a person.*
OPPOSITE *Only after years of sequestered training in a secret society will Yacouba stilt dancers perform before their village.*

of West African trade routes from inland across the desert to towards the coast. Timbuktu was initially a Tuareg settlement and means 'place of Buktu' – Buktu being a woman who tended Tuareg animals while the men were away. Although it was originally known as an area of wealth, the failure of early explorers to report on Timbuktu changed its meaning to a place at the end of the earth – a term used even today.

Two hundred and fifty kilometres (160 miles) south of Mali's city of Timbuktu are the massive Bandiagara Cliffs, a spectacular series of massive cliffs 135 kilometres (84 miles) long and up to 80 storeys high. On and around the cliffs dwell an ancient people called the Dogon, who for nearly 600 years have used the cliffs as a sanctuary against marauding peoples. Virtually untouched by Western culture, the Dogon retain their traditional way of living, including making blood sacrifices to their gods and ancestors.

Like the Tellem people who resided along the Bandiagara centuries ago, the Dogon also bury their deceased in caves high in the cliffs. The Dogon revere their dead as they are believed to form an intermediary step between them and their first ancestors, who are their gods. Everything is symbolic to the Dogon, linking the spiritual and real worlds.

From the top of the Bandiagara Escarpment, villages far below look like miniature models. The Dogon live on a precipice figuratively and literally; for them, as well as the other people of the Sahel, their lives depend on a short rainy season which occasionally fails. This total dependency on the rains has not helped Mali

LEFT *Typical of the colour and vibrancy of West African markets is the weekly market held at the ancient town of Djenné in Mali.*

emerge from being one of the world's poorest countries, a position shared by neighbours Burkina Faso and Niger.

Niger, like Nigeria, takes its name from the Niger River. Starting less than 300 kilometres (190 miles) from the sea, the 4 180-kilometre-long (2 600 miles) river heads inland as far as Timbuktu and Gão before flowing southeast through Niger on its journey to the sea. Along with Mali and southern Algeria, Niger is home to the nomadic Tuareg people. Their nickname 'the Blue Men of the Desert' comes from their robes and *tagilmusts* (turbans), often dyed in natural indigo which rubs off on their skin.

A few Tuaregs cling to their traditional way of life. Large camel caravans still occasionally cross the desert, usually to and from distant salt mines such as the remote settlements of Bilma in eastern Niger and Taoudenni in northern Mali. More common are smaller camel trains, especially around places like Niger's Agadez which has a camel market. The town has been important in trans-Saharan trade for centuries, and is famous for its leatherwork and silver jewellery. Particular to Niger are silver crosses, the designs of which represent specific desert towns.

Through hardships of climate, slavery, drought and disease, West Africans have retained their traditions and culture, and a vibrancy for life. Stories of sultans, castles, cliff-dwellers and desert caravans are real, not only in the distant past but alive even today.

OPPOSITE *Bororo nomads (also called Wodaabe) of the Niger region draw attention to themselves by wearing elaborate jewellery.*
RIGHT *Adornment is also very important to Peul women (part of the larger Fulani ethnic group) and may include facial tattoos, gold and silver jewellery and old silver coins.*

VISIONS OF AFRICA

PREVIOUS PAGES *The lunar landscape of Roumsiki in northern Cameroon is part of a chain of volcanoes that begins nearly 2 000 kilometres (1 243 miles) away in the Indian Ocean.*

ABOVE *Traditional methods of building bridges using vines are still used near Memfe in Cameroon.*

RIGHT *Ceremonial pipers at the Sultan's Palace at Foumban, Cameroon, announce the arrival of the Sultan.*

FOLLOWING PAGES *Boats tie up at St George's Castle in Elmina, Ghana, where fishing, rather than slavery as before, is now the town's main industry.*

LEFT *Remnants of British colonial buildings slowly crumble at the fishing village of Dixcove in Ghana.*

ABOVE *The Crab Sorcerer in Roumsiki, northern Cameroon, hums and sings to a musical instrument which makes the crabs in his clay pot move. He then divines the future according to the position of the crabs in the pot.*

FOLLOWING PAGES *Few mosques in West Africa are as impressive as the one at Mali's Djenné. Wooden reinforcement doubles as external scaffolding used in annual plastering.*

LEFT *Although Islam spread across the Sahel 1 000 years ago and dominates the region, some areas are still strongly animist and converts like this village elder in western Ivory Coast are in the minority.*

BELOW *Agadez, on the southern fringes of the Sahara Desert in Niger, is known for the hand-made silver jewellery it produces, and for its mosque, built in the Sudanic mud architecture style typical of the Sahel.*

OPPOSITE *Rebuilt about a century ago, the original mud mosque at Djenné in Mali dates back to the 11th century.*

PREVIOUS PAGES *The Dan people of the Ivory Coast are famed for their stilt dancing,*
which involves acrobatic tumbling to accompanying rhythmic drumming. Entertainers
perform at village ceremonies, for tourists and sometimes in travelling troupes.
ABOVE *Introduced around 2 000 years ago, camels proved to be ideal beasts of*
burden in the arid Sahara and Sahel regions.
OPPOSITE *For centuries the Dogon, and before them the Tellem people, have*
buried their dead in tombs high in the cliffs above villages dotted along Mali's
135-kilometre-long (84 miles) Bandiagara Escarpment.

EAST AFRICA

East Africa is best known for its teeming wildlife, and it is here in the great game parks of the Serengeti in Tanzania and its neighbour, the Masai Mara in Kenya, that the quintessential African landscapes are found. Vast plains dotted with flat-topped acacia trees are home to a greater abundance and variety of wildlife than anywhere else in the world.

The 'hunt' that takes television documentaries months and even years to capture on film is played out every day in East Africa's game parks. Among the predators are the large cats – lion, leopard and cheetah – as well as hyena, jackal and the rare African wild dog. Prey is plentiful, especially during the annual mass migration when an estimated one and a half million wildebeest follow the rains to fresh pastures between the Serengeti plains and the Masai Mara reserve. A chain of shallow lakes in Kenya is home to birdlife that also numbers in the millions: flamingos are so prolific that lakes are tinged pink. Much less numerous, but just as impressive are the mountain gorillas found in the rainforests in the border regions of the Democratic Republic of Congo (formerly Zaïre), Rwanda and Uganda.

But East Africa offers more than just superb wildlife. Its landscapes are magnificent, with mighty rivers like the Nile and valleys such as the Rift, and it embraces the continent's largest lakes and highest mountains. The region also boasts a long and fascinating history.

PREVIOUS PAGES *The Congo River, lifeline to thousands of people in the Congo Basin.*
OPPOSITE *Gondar in the Ethiopian Highlands is home to a series of castles built by emperors three and a half centuries ago.*
RIGHT *Facial tattoos are sometimes seen on Christian women in the Ethiopian Highlands.*

For around 25 centuries a remote mountain kingdom existed thousands of metres high in the Ethiopian Highlands. The kingdom lost its 225th and last monarch when Emperor Hailé Selassié died in 1975. Hailé Selassié was also considered a god to Rastafarians, who take their name from his former name Ras (a title of princes and governors) Tafari. Ethiopian legend dates the monarchy back to around 1000BC when Ethiopia's Queen of Sheba bore Israel's King Solomon a son, Menelik, who became the country's first Emperor. Menelik is reputed to have smuggled the Ark of the Covenant (containing the Ten Commandments) from Jerusalem to Ethiopia. The Ark is central to the Ethiopian form of Christianity, with more than 20 000 representations in churches around the country. It is claimed that the original is still held in the St Mary of Zion Church at Axum, an ancient capital in the north of Ethiopia.

Axum was one of the world's most powerful civilizations during the middle of the first millennium AD, when it ruled parts of the

Middle East as well as trading as far afield as Greece, Rome and India. One of Axum's most intriguing sights are its huge stone stelae and obelisks. The largest stele still standing is seven storeys tall and was erected around 400AD. Cut from a quarry 5 kilometres (3 miles) away, the transport and erection of the 150-tonne-block of stone remains a mystery.

South of Axum lies the remote mountain village of Lalibela. The town, another ancient capital of Ethiopia, is cut off for several months a year when the rainy season washes away its rough access track. At Lalibela Africa is left behind and a scene reminiscent of the Bible is entered. On Saturdays people from the surrounding countryside stream into town for the weekly market. Dressed in beige robes, with their donkeys or camels carrying goods, lines of people come to trade livestock and *amoles*, or bars of salt – until recently still used as a currency. Small piles of a grey, powdery resin (frankincense and myrrh) are sold beside fossilized resin (amber) and silver jewellery.

The market scene appears unchanged from 800 years ago when Lalibela was in its prime, and when, according to legend, an angel carved 11 enormous stone churches out of solid bedrock. Although the legend may not be true, astonishingly the 8-century-old churches are not only real but still in daily use with the floors, columns and roofs all carved, rather than built, from a single piece of rock. Descending to a subterranean world, passages and tunnels connect many of these monolithic churches. In dimly lit cavernous interiors, rows of priests swing bronze censers that burn pungent myrrh. The dank, primeval odour combined with the priests' hypnotic chant seem to belong to another time and place. In Lalibela even the cafés, with their straw-covered floors, incense-laden air and often resident livestock, seem like a nativity scene from the Bible.

It is said that Ethiopia slept for a thousand years, and even today little is known about the country's isolated highlands. The mountain kingdom has certainly had minimal influence from the outside world, developing its own alphabet, religion, cuisine and written language – it even uses an alternative calendar. Animals have also evolved in isolation, with species like the gelada baboon, Simien fox and Walia ibex found nowhere else in the world.

Preconceived ideas and stereotypes of a barren, flat, dusty landscape disappear at the edge of the Ethiopian lowlands where roads zigzag skywards to the highlands, three vertical kilometres (2 miles) above. Although some parts of Ethiopia do consist of drought-prone desert, the highlands receive more rain than most of Europe and contribute 85 percent of the water for Egypt's mighty Nile River via the Blue Nile. The run-off between the highlands and the Blue Nile is so great that it has carved a massive void in the earth's surface: the Blue Nile Gorge is up to 1.5 kilometres (1 mile) deep and 25 kilometres (15 miles) wide, and is so steep and inaccessible that it was not until the 1960s that it was fully explored with the aid of helicopters. Some of the unusual discoveries found in the gorge were a cave containing dozens of mummies, and an enormous trench hundreds of kilometres long – both finds have unknown origins.

The Blue Nile's major source is in Ethiopia's Lake Tana which has a surface area of some 3 600 square kilometres (1 400 square miles). Dozens of islands are found in the lake, some

OPPOSITE *A village chief in Ethiopia – a country whose name means 'burnt faces'.*
RIGHT *Heavy rains and steep topography in the Simien Mountains in Ethiopia make seasonal flash floods common.*

105

of which are home to monasteries over 600 years old. Just 30 kilometres (20 miles) from Lake Tana's outlet, the Blue Nile plunges over a sheer cliff face to form Tissisat ('smoke of fire') Falls. In 1770 Scottish Explorer James Bruce described them as '...they fell in one sheet of water, without any interval, above half an English Mile in breadth, with a force and noise that was truly terrible, and which stunned and made me for a time, perfectly dizzy'. As with many early explorers, Bruce's (accurate) descriptions were ridiculed in Europe. In the dry season the falls are only a fraction of their wet season flow.

North of Tissisat Falls lies yet another ancient Ethiopian capital, Gondar. In the centre of the town is a compound of castles, some of which date back over three and a half centuries – modern by Ethiopian standards.

Although Ethiopia's section of the Nile is impressive, it cannot be compared to the flow of another African river, the Congo. About 2 000 kilometres (1 200 miles) shorter than the Nile, the Congo River in the Congo (Kinshasa) is immense in anyone's terms. In places it is more than 20 kilometres (12 miles) wide and flows 4 670 kilometres (2 900 miles) from its source, draining water from an area nearly 15 times the size of Great Britain. Where it eventually enters the Atlantic Ocean it has carved a trench in the ocean floor that is up to 150 kilometres (95 miles) long and up to 2 kilometres (1.25 miles) deep.

The enormous river forms such a barrier that it may have caused the evolution of a separate species of the chimpanzee. Bonobos are found exclusively on the left bank of the Congo River, while the closest population of chimpanzees live on the right bank.

In a region with a very wet climate, the main roads are often impassable for weeks on end as they consist of dirt tracks only. A road that is

closed because of a common problem like broken bridges can be reclaimed in a matter of weeks by the brooding rainforest. Attempts at modernization – communication systems, factories, roads and other infrastructures – have been largely thwarted by the forest.

From Joseph Conrad's 19th-century novel *Heart of Darkness* and Henry Morton Stanley's explorations, the Congo Basin's rainforest has been brought to life as a mysterious, evil power. Stanley was peppered by poisoned arrows thrown by some 2 000 cannibals from flotillas of dugout canoes. Today dugout canoes (pirogues) trade with barges and riverboats that ply the Congo River and its tributaries. When the riverboats and attendant barges are running, they can become floating cities of 5 000 or more people.

The pirogues, some up to 30 metres (100 feet) in length, are tied up to the riverboats with liana vines, and live domestic animals – pigs, goats and chickens – are unloaded onto the boats. Other live wild animals from the forest – crocodiles, turtles and big green speckled monitor lizards over a metre long (40 inches) – are taken aboard the busy floating markets, either to be sold or eaten. Two-metre-long (6.5 feet) catfish with bodies as thick as a human torso are also loaded aboard, as well as snakes, smoked monkeys, dried fish and chimpanzees, the latter kept as pets or guard animals. Pirogues stacked high with bamboo furniture and mats are unloaded beside others filled with tropical fruit and produce from the forest.

The Congo River is the lifeline to millions of people who live in the Congo Basin. Together with its tributaries, some of which are even longer than 2 000 kilometres (1 200 miles), this vast river system provides more than 14 000 kilometres (8 700 miles) of navigable waterways. In the Congo Basin, the river is one

of the few places where the claustrophobic rainforest can be escaped. Many locals have a deep suspicion of the forest, clearing it well back to set up their dwellings, but an exception to this are the Pygmies.

Although known collectively to outsiders as Pygmies (a term derived from a Greek word meaning the distance from the knuckles to the elbow), Pygmies themselves do not like this label and prefer to be called by their individual ethnic name, or in one dialect *bamiki ba ndura* – children of the forest. Their short stature is an advantage in moving swiftly and silently through the forest's thick undergrowth.

The hunter-gatherer lifestyle of the Pygmies and their intimate knowledge of the rainforest enables them to survive there in a semi-nomadic manner, living off the forest's bounty of wild nuts and berries, mushrooms, honey and wild game. Other people can only survive here by destroying the fragile environment. To protect their forest (which some groups call 'mother') Pygmies will sometimes virtually enslave themselves to those living around the fringes. The Pygmies often work the fields of the outsiders for very low wages, and sometimes sell forest products, such as honey and nuts, to them. To some extent this helps keep the outsiders out of the forest who thus, with a slightly increased standard of living, do then not need to slash and burn to increase the size of their fields.

Huts of the Pygmies are made of a circle of sticks inserted into the ground and bent inwards to form an igloo shape. Tiled in large forest leaves, the huts are built in a very short time and serve as home for a few weeks before

OPPOSITE *Not far from its major source of Lake Tana in the Ethiopian Highlands, the Blue Nile forms the dramatic Tissisat Falls.*

they rot back into the forest floor. Hunting methods differ from clan to clan, some using bow and poisoned arrow, others using long tennis-like nets which are laid out in the rainforest to catch small forest antelope.

Perhaps the most famous inhabitants of tropical Africa's rainforests are the gorillas. Although western lowland gorillas can be found on the west coast of tropical Africa (in small numbers), it is the rare and endangered eastern gorillas that have captured the world's attention. The two types of eastern gorilla are the mountain gorilla, living in high rainforests in the Virunga Mountains around the border regions of Uganda, Rwanda and the Congo (Kinshasa), and the very similar eastern lowland gorilla which lives nearby in eastern Congo. Both have become very popular with tourists. Ironically, it is publicity from Dian Fossey's book and the subsequent film *Gorillas in the Mist* that have brought the tourists that the late Ms Fossey so detested. However, because of tourism the gorillas have become a valuable local commodity, worth more alive than dead. Along with the work of dedicated individuals and groups, tourism, therefore, is staving off extinction for the gorillas for the time being.

Few wildlife experiences compare to visiting the gorillas. After trekking sometimes for several hours, small guided groups come face to face with a family of gorillas on their own turf. The dominant male or 'silverback' often weighs more than 200 kilograms (440 pounds), and has eyes that seem to understand and convey expressions, and hands that work the same as human's. At seven times our own

LEFT *Dugout canoes, or pirogues, like this one on the Congo River, can take up to half a year to be carved from a single tree.*

strength, the massive silverback should be treated with great respect, especially when only a mere 2 metres (6.5 feet) away. It is a wildlife experience that evokes excitement, fear, compassion and awe – and often leads the viewer to sit dumbstruck before the enormous beast. In recent years civil unrest has made the region very volatile, with areas becoming unsafe for people and gorillas for long periods.

From the gorillas' home in the Virunga Mountains around a degree south of the equator, it is not far to the Ruwenzori Mountains, which are just half a degree north of the equator on the Ugandan/Congo (Kinshasa) border. The source of much rumour and speculation for centuries, the Ruwenzoris, or 'Mountains of the Moon', were virtually unknown until Stanley's 'discovery' in 1888. One of his expedition team members had actually seen the mountains a month before, but Stanley had dismissed the discovery. Several explorers had passed by their base in previous years (including Stanley) and some had seen a 'distant blue mass'; one had even glimpsed their snowy peaks but only wrote about it privately for fear of ridicule.

The Ruwenzoris (a local name meaning 'rainmaker') rise to 5 109 metres (16 760 feet), and the steamy forest below gives way to various stages of alpine vegetation. Although in tropical Africa, the top of the massif consists of a series of permanent ice caps, glaciers, snow and rocky peaks, forming a world as unlike Africa as most people could imagine. Unusual vegetation grows at lower levels, such as giant lobelias and groundsels many times their normal size. In the 'enchanted forest', so called because of its almost fairytale look with lichens dangling through thick mist, a hollow false floor is formed by a tangle of tree roots carpeted by soft green mosses.

Below the Ruwenzori Mountains on the Ugandan side lies one of the most varied wildlife parks on the whole African continent. The Queen Elizabeth National Park boasts

ABOVE *The mountain gorilla is only found in a few small, isolated family groups in the Great Lakes region of East Africa.*
RIGHT *Using a wooden scooter, a boy carts a load of spring onions to market in eastern Congo's Vurunga Mountains.*

vegetation ranging from open grassland plains to thick tropical forest, home to species like chimpanzee and monkey. The Ishasha River end of the park is one of the few places where lions regularly climb trees, while at the Ruwenzori side are over 80 volcanic craters up to 3 kilometres (2 miles) across, some with

their own lakes. Dissecting the park and running between Lakes Edward and George, is the Kazinga Channel which supports a vast number of hippo. Elephant and buffalo are common visitors to the channel, while fish eagles, pelicans, herons and storks are among the abundant birdlife that live alongside it, contributing to the approximately 500 bird species that can be seen in the park.

North of the Queen Elizabeth Park lies Murchison Falls National Park. Once home to teeming wildlife, the park had most of its game exterminated during Uganda's brutal dictatorships of the 1970s and early '80s. However, one of its major attractions remains unspoilt. At Murchison Falls, the Victoria Nile River narrows to just 6 metres (20 feet) and launches itself through a gap to plummet violently over several steps, until finally it again becomes a calm, wide river far below. In well over 6 000 kilometres (3 700 miles) it is here that the Nile is most impressive, showing a power so awesome that reverberations can be felt through the ground and air – and a noise so thunderous that it drowns out all speech.

On the banks of the Victoria Nile below Murchison Falls lie enormous Nile crocodiles, fattened by the numerous fish that tumble over the falls. Hippo wallow in the calmer waters while birdlife, including the strange and very rare whale-headed (shoebill) stork, live along the banks. The major source of the Victoria, Albert and White Nile rivers is the outlet of Lake Victoria at Jinja in Uganda. The lake, shared by Uganda, Tanzania and Kenya, is the world's second largest freshwater lake.

LEFT *Tanzania's and Africa's highest mountain, Mount Kilimanjaro, provides the perfect scenic backdrop for a herd of elephants in Kenya's Amboseli National Park.*

On the far side of Lake Victoria in Tanzania is one of the world's most famous game parks – the Serengeti National Park (*siringet* is Maasai for wide open space). Its vast grasslands are home to some of the biggest herds of plains game on the continent. From around December until May over a million wildebeest spread across the Serengeti plains to calve and take advantage of good pasture from the rains. When the region dries out the wildebeest, as well as Thompson's gazelle and zebra, move north in a dramatic mass migration towards Kenya's Masai Mara National Reserve.

Much of the Serengeti plains lie outside the national park, but within the Ngorongoro Conservation Area. As the area is not a national park (generally the highest classification affording the most protection that a country can give to a game reserve or natural area), it has different rules which, while still protecting wildlife, allow local Maasai people to graze and water their cattle.

The Ngorongoro Conservation Area also encompasses Ngorongoro Crater, which is a caldera, or collapsed volcano. Around 2.5 million years ago – a million years after early humanoids left their footprints at nearby Laetoli – the top of the then volcanic cone collapsed inwards, dropping around two and a half vertical kilometres (1.5 miles).

Today the crater is home to an abundance of wildlife and birdlife. Permanent springs and lakes in its 20-kilometre-wide (12.5 miles) floor and its 600-metre-high (1 970 feet) walls provide a permanent and virtually inescapable home to 25 000 to 30 000 mammals. The crater contains most of the major mammal species of the East African plains but a notable exception are giraffe, possibly because the crater's small forest is not big enough to support them. It is one of the best places to see the endangered black rhino, but cheetah and leopard are usually absent due to a high concentration of lion and hyena, although leopard thrive on the cool, forested crater rim.

East of Ngorongoro Crater, near the Kenyan border, lies another of Tanzania's spectacular volcanoes, or more correctly three volcanoes. Together they form Mount Kilimanjaro – at 5 895 metres (19 340 feet) it is Africa's highest mountain. When German Johannes Rebmann first set his eyes on the permanent snow and icefields of Kilimanjaro in 1848, his reports were laughed at in Europe. Even today, from the steamy tropical forest at Kilimanjaro's base, it is difficult to imagine the Arctic-like conditions at the peak, usually hidden in clouds five vertical kilometres (3 miles) above.

Another of Tanzania's famed landmarks is 'the spice island' of Zanzibar. The 'Tan' in Tanganyika (the lake and previously the country) along with the 'Zan' in Zanzibar made up the name Tanzania when the two territories joined in 1964. For centuries this exotic island has been a crossroads of cultures and a major trading post between India, the Middle East and Africa.

Today this mix of peoples is reflected in the Swahili ('coastal') culture. The Swahili language was born from a need by Arab slave traders to communicate with their captives. Probably the most famous Swahili word is safari. Literally meaning 'journey', safari has come to mean a specific type of journey, usually to a game park.

Further up the East African coast, Kenya's island of Lamu is similar in many ways to Zanzibar. One major difference – the absence of roads or vehicles – contributes to the island's very relaxed atmosphere, and has made it popular with travellers. The main 'street' is less than 2 metres (6.5 feet) wide in places, and the biggest hazard for unwary tourists is being knocked over by a donkey.

Adding to the restful mood is the sight of wooden dhows, still built traditionally by hand, sailing lazily along the coast.

Another of Kenya's prime tourist areas is the Masai Mara National Reserve, and few game parks anywhere in Africa can match it for proliferation of game. The Masai Mara reserve adjoins Tanzania's Serengeti National Park and belongs to the same ecosystem, forming the northern section of the annual wildebeest migration. Virtually all East African plains game species can be found in this one park – lions are numerous, as are zebra, giraffe and elephant.

Around the Masai Mara live the Maasai people. Unusually tall and slim, these proud cattle-herding people make up a small but conspicuous part of Kenya's population. Their stretched earlobes, spears, red cloaks and ochre-coloured hair make them unmistakable as they graze their cattle on open grassland plains. With a diet that includes a mix of cows' blood and milk, and an initiation rite (which until recently included killing a lion) for entry to an age-based warrior class, Maasai have become the quintessential African warriors to the tourists who daily pass through their area.

In the north of Kenya the Samburu have a similar culture to their Maasai cousins. They speak a slightly different version of the Maa language but are thought to be part of the same ethnic group that originally came from the Sudan. They are also tall and slim and wear beaded jewellery, although Samburu girls prefer multiple strings of necklaces rather than the flat, beaded collars of the Maasai.

Another allied ethnic group, once called the smallest group in Africa (numerically), are the El Molo. Living on the edge of Lake Turkana,

OPPOSITE *An olive baboon in Lake Manyara National Park, Tanzania.*

the El Molo are regarded as inferior by some of their neighbours as they have no cattle. Instead they are fishermen, but are so few in numbers that they are gradually being assimilated into the much larger cattle-herding Samburu.

The area around Lake Turkana has a very harsh environment, and burning winds are not uncommon across the almost vegetationless region. Even the lake is hostile to humans – it supports numerous fish species, but its waters are very alkaline and crawling with crocodiles. To the east of the lake stretches the vast, empty Chalbi Desert.

Like Lake Turkana, other Rift Valley lakes in Kenya are also highly alkaline (hence their common name of soda lakes) and support large numbers of greater and lesser flamingos. The best known example is Lake Nakuru, in Lake Nakuru National Park, which turns pink when up to two million flamingos settle on its waters. As is the case in some of the other shallow Rift Valley lakes, the levels of algae on which the flamingos feed fluctuate due to salt levels. Because of this, flamingos will often fly to another lake where conditions are better. Apart from flamingos and numerous pelicans, the park is home to another 400 bird species.

East Africa's large variety of landscapes in a way compares to its diverse wildlife. It has some of the world's wettest and driest regions, Africa's highest mountains and lowest depressions, massive volcanoes and calderas, enormous lakes and rivers. Vegetation ranges from tropical rainforests to barren deserts. And its wildlife has adapted to almost all of these conditions to give what is perhaps nature's greatest show on earth.

RIGHT *Looking out over the vast savanna in Kenya are these Maasai warriors, or moran, typically wearing red cloaks.*

LEFT *Frankincense, myrrh, silver, salt and camels are traded at Lalibela market in a scene reminiscent of ancient times.*

ABOVE *Many roads in the Ethiopian Highlands pass through high mountain passes and spectacular landscape, such as this scene viewed from the road to Lalibela.*

FOLLOWING PAGES *Flamingos, seen here on Lake Bogoria in Kenya, suck in water through fringed brushes, filtering out the algae on which they feed.*

LEFT *This village market in the Congo Basin faces the Congo River, connecting it to over 14 000 kilometres (8 700 miles) of navigable waterways.*
ABOVE *In some parts of Africa, like the Congo Basin, women's hairstyles have been raised to an art form. In other areas of the continent, beads, old silver coins, hair extensions, butterfat or ochre are added to hair to enhance beauty.*

ABOVE *Decoration is very important to the Maasai of Tanzania and Kenya. They have over 40 words to describe their elaborate beads, and shave their heads to draw attention to themselves.*

RIGHT *Traditional medicine still plays a large part in many African cultures. This witch doctor belongs to the Kikuyu ethnic group, the largest of more than 70 such groups in Kenya.*

EAST AFRICA

LEFT   The beautiful, solitary and mainly nocturnal leopard, like this one at the Serengeti National Park in Tanzania, is seldom seen but is present in a large variety of habitats ranging from virtual desert to rainforest.

BELOW   The reticulated giraffe is one of seven or eight giraffe subspecies, each with a different pattern or colour and distribution. This lovely animal is a resident of the Masai Mara National Reserve in Kenya.

FOLLOWING PAGES Elephants come to drink at a waterhole near Voi Game Lodge, East Tsavo National Park in Kenya. Until a young elephant learns to use the trunk's 100 000 muscles, the trunk often moves around out of control and the youngster has to go down on bended knees to drinks with its mouth.

127

LEFT *Narrow, crooked alleys, overhanging balconies and elaborately carved brass-studded doors give the Old Stone Town in Zanzibar a deservedly exotic reputation. This Tanzanian Indian Ocean island has been a trading base between Africa, the Middle East and India for over 1 000 years, and is known for its spices, seafood, tropical fruit and old Arab dhows.*

ABOVE *Uganda is dogged and often stereotyped by its turbulent past, but Ugandans are renowned as being warm and friendly people who live in a fertile, lush country.*

SOUTHERN AFRICA

A region of mostly dry, flat bushland, Southern Africa is punctuated by some of the most breathtaking scenery in the world. 'Scenes so lovely must have been gazed upon by Angels in their flight' wrote intrepid explorer Doctor David Livingstone about Victoria Falls. But the magnificence of Southern Africa embraces much more than the Falls.

The great orange dunes of the Namib Desert are so large that it is difficult to comprehend their proportions. This is also true of the Fish River Canyon, a spectacularly deep abyss that twists like a serpent for some 160 kilometres (100 miles) through southern Namibia. From the oven-like temperatures in the depths of the canyon, the climate change could hardly be more extreme when compared with some of Southern Africa's lofty mountain ranges: when covered in snow, South Africa's Drakensberg seems not only un-African but the landscape appears almost unworldly.

In Botswana further contrast exists: although virtually surrounded by desert, the Okavango, the world's largest inland delta, is alive with plants and animals thriving in a verdant area of islands and water. Similarly, the cool, lush Eastern Highlands in Zimbabwe are more like parts of Europe than the hot, dry plains which lie to their south. As well as superb scenery, Southern Africa also boasts some of the world's best game parks, rivalled only by those in East Africa, and offers unexpected treasures in a region of incredible diversity.

PREVIOUS PAGES *The spectacular Victoria Falls is shared by Zimbabwe and Zambia.* OPPOSITE *Lake Malawi provides plentiful catches for fishermen in dugout canoes.* RIGHT *The Himba of Namibia remain relatively untouched by Western civilization.*

Bordered by Mozambique and Tanzania, Lake Malawi forms 20 percent of Malawi's territory. When missionary-explorer David Livingstone first saw Lake Malawi on his 1866 trip, he used its local name 'Nyasa' which means 'lake'. Subsequently the country also took the name Nyasa until it gained independence in 1961, when its name was changed to Malawi.

Lake Malawi has more fish species than any other body of fresh water in the world and its 200 or so endemic species indicate that the lake has been separated from other large bodies of water for a very long time. The lake is one of the most picturesque in Africa, and a combination of clean, clear waters with few hippos or crocodiles makes it popular for swimming. One of the best places to see the fish is at Lake Malawi National Park at Cape Maclear. The park was one of the world's first underwater parks in a freshwater lake and has been declared a World Heritage Site. Here the

majestic African fish eagle is a common sight in trees overlooking the lake, and its haunting, shrill cry is unforgettable.

Atop an escarpment high above Lake Malawi lies the small village of Livingstonia. In the village church, stained glass windows depict scenes from Doctor David Livingstone's travels, but Livingstone never saw the village. It was set up in his memory, 21 years after his death in 1873.

One escarpment Livingstone did climb is the one to Zomba Plateau. The plateau now has plantation forestry as well as its original indigenous forests, and trout fill Zomba's streams. Separated around much of its circumference by sheer cliffs, cool, lush Zomba transcends the surrounding hot lowlands. Likewise, the Mulanje massif in Malawi's south dominates an area of tea plantations; the massive granite outcrop rises nearly 2 kilometres (1.25 miles) to domed peaks interspersed with hiking tracks.

Across Malawi's border lies Zambia which takes its name from the Zambezi River. Zambia boasts one of Africa's most underrated wildlife regions – North and South Luangwa national parks. With few tracks or visitors, these parks offer plentiful wildlife and a more unspoilt wildlife experience than many of Africa's more popular parks. Crocodiles and hippos are particularly numerous along the Luangwa River, and for long stretches, pods of several dozen hippo can be seen every 50 or 100 metres (165 or 330 feet).

Another of Zambia's national parks is Kafue, one of Africa's largest reserves with a national park status. Kafue has hardly any tracks and is very much a wilderness area but some areas of the park provide excellent game-viewing.

Zambia's neighbour to the southeast is Zimbabwe, with the Zambezi River forming a boundary between the two countries. Without a doubt both Zimbabwe's and Zambia's most magnificent natural feature is Victoria Falls, one of the Seven Natural Wonders of the World. When one is approaching the Falls, the first inkling that something spectacular lies ahead can be noticed as far as 20 kilometres (12 miles) away as a great cloud of spray rises high into the sky looking deceptively like smoke from a massive bush fire. From here until Victoria Falls, little except the rising spray can be seen. It is not until you are just 50 metres (165 feet) from the face of the Falls that their full splendour can be appreciated.

In a deafening roar, the Zambezi River plummets in a virtually continous sheet of water 1.5 kilometres (1 mile) long, over a 30-storey-high bluff. The Falls drop into an immense fissure – a weak line in the earth's surface – before flowing out a narrow gap and zigzagging down a series of nearly parallel fissures, each one a previous and progressively older Victoria Falls.

Local people had their own names for Victoria Falls before David Livingstone named them. *Mosi-oa-Tunya* ('The Smoke that Thunders') was the Makololo name, while the Tonga people called them *Shongwe* ('Seething Cauldron'). Aircraft and helicopter trips – appropriately named 'Flight of the Angels' – is the only way to see the Falls in their entirety, showing the deceptively calm Zambezi River above the Falls and the big, turbulent rapids, used for white-water rafting, in the Batoka Gorge downstream.

In the 1950s the river was dammed at Kariba to form Lake Kariba – the largest man-made lake in the world at the time. The

RIGHT *The ancient ruins of Great Zimbabwe have fuelled many legends, and have also given the country of Zimbabwe its name.*

280-kilometre-long (174 miles) lake is said to contain enough crocodiles to lie head to tail and encircle the lake's shoreline three and a half times. However, calculated estimates put Kariba's crocodile population at a 'mere' 20 000 to 30 000.

Downstream from Kariba lies the unspoilt Mana Pools National Park. Situated on the flood plain of the Zambezi, Mana (meaning 'four') Pools is unusual in that visitors are allowed to get out of their vehicles and walk around unguided – in a park where lion, elephant, buffalo and hippo are common.

At Hwange National Park in the west of Zimbabwe, large herds of elephant are so numerous that they have become a problem, destroying vegetation to such an extent that other wildlife has become affected. While Mana Pools is left very much to itself, Hwange and several other parks in Southern Africa have strong policies of wildlife management and control. Artificial waterholes provide good viewing for tourists and enable the park to sustain higher levels of wildlife – an advantage with the ever-increasing human demands for land which puts pressure on wildlife outside park boundaries. While not totally natural, many parks that employ wildlife management have been successful in their goals and overall conservation of wildlife.

The Matobo National Park, in the Matobo Hills near Bulawayo, is known as much for its unusual rock formations and ancient San (Bushmen) cave paintings as for its wildlife. Steep, wooded, rocky hills with granite outcrops provide the perfect hunting ground for a large population of leopard, although they are seldom seen because of the animals'

LEFT *Zimbabwe's Mana Pools National Park supports a rich variety of wildlife.*

secretive nature, and because of the landscape. The park is also a stronghold for a small population of black and white rhino, and the majestic black eagle.

Zimbabwe's name – meaning 'stone houses' – was taken from the once grand mediaeval city and Southern Africa's greatest ancient ruins, Great Zimbabwe. Enormous drystone walls at Great Zimbabwe form two major complexes. Consisting of a massive circular wall up to 5 metres (16 feet) thick is the Great Enclosure, while high above on a strategic outcrop lies the Hill Complex. Pathways and passages lead between the walls and natural rock formations, giving the appearance of a fortress. Great Zimbabwe is steeped in mystery, largely because of a lack of written records and facts about the place.

From its prime around 1500, it began to decline. The most popular theory for this is that the city was a victim of its own success, and it broke up into factions after the local resources failed to support some 10 000 Karanga people. As well as Great Zimbabwe, there are another 150 sites of ruins in Zimbabwe.

In the east of Zimbabwe lie the evocative Eastern Highlands, made up of three distinct regions. Chimanimani, the southern section, is a mountainous wilderness area with streams, waterfalls, caves and several hiking tracks. Mount Binga, the highest point (2 437 metres; 7 995 feet) in the Chimanimani National Park, lies on Mozambique's border and is also the highest point in Mozambique.

The Bvumba Mountains form the central part of the Eastern Highlands which, like Chimanimani, have a cool and often misty climate (Bvumba means 'mist'). With botanic gardens, colonial-styled hotels, luxuriant vegetation and abundant birdlife throughout its forests, as well as a refreshing climate, the Bvumba could be part of Scotland or Wales.

The dams and streams of the third region, Nyanga, are popular with trout fishermen, and its mountains, including Zimbabwe's highest – Mount Inyangani at 2 592 metres (8 500 feet) – offer outstanding walking and hiking trails. Nyanga has several waterfalls, including the Mtarazi Falls – one of the world's highest. Although the water flow is small, it plunges off the edge of a vertical escarpment into the Honde Valley 750 metres (2 460 feet) below.

To the east of the Eastern Highlands lies Mozambique, recovering from a long civil war. The country has great tourism potential with its natural attributes of a massive 2 500 kilometres (1 550 miles) of coastline which is peppered with white sandy beaches, palm trees, coral reefs and offshore tropical islands. Abundant marine life inhabits its clear, warm waters, providing excellent deep sea fishing, while the islands of the Bazaruto Archipelago, where there is a fine marine reserve, offer superb diving and snorkelling.

Away from the coast and in the centre of Southern Africa, Botswana is in total contrast to Zimbabwe's cool Eastern Highlands or Mozambique's idyllic beaches. Vast salt pans – the Makgadikgadi Pans – cover large areas of Botswana's Kalahari Desert, and are remnants of what was once Africa's largest lake. Ironically, the pans are now in one of the continent's driest regions, although from time to time they flood, attracting thousands of flamingos – in stark contrast to their normal glaringly white, crusty surface.

In the Makgadikgadi and Nxai Pan National Park are Baines' Baobabs. Made famous in a painting by Thomas Baines over a hundred years ago, these prehistoric-looking trees have changed little in the ensuing century.

A lack of permanent water over much of Botswana's territory means that large tracts of land are uninhabitable and left as wilderness areas. Although most people (except perhaps for the San) are unable to survive here, it does not mean that wildlife cannot. A number of animals, such as zebra, gemsbok and lion, have adapted to the dry conditions, moving to well-watered areas as the seasons change.

Chobe National Park in Botswana's north forms part of an ecosystem that extends into other parts of Botswana, as well as Zambia, Zimbabwe, Namibia and Angola. Wildlife, particularly elephants, migrate between regions and at times there can be over 70 000 elephants in Chobe. Several permanent water sources feed the vast ecosystem. Chobe National Park is watered by the Chobe River, and by the Zambezi which is not far away. To the west is the Okavango River – the lifeblood of one of the world's most unique wildlife refuges.

The Okavango Delta is an enormous inland swamp that supports vast numbers of wildlife. The typical way to journey around the Delta's 15 000-square kilometre (5 790-square mile) myriad of waterways is to be poled along in a dugout canoe, or *makoro*; there can be few more pleasant or tranquil ways of travelling, and visitors are unlikely to find the waterways and islands overcrowded, except perhaps by birdlife. As game-viewing usually takes place from a *mokoro* or on foot, vantage points are lower and distance covered less than when travelling in a vehicle. Because of this, wildlife can sometimes appear to be scarce, but game proliferates in the Okavango Delta and can easily be seen on an aerial game flight.

Several kilometres from the Delta, across the desert that nearly encircles it, the dry air gives way to the irresistible scent of water, of life. So immense is the Delta that the majority of its water is lost to evaporation. What water is left seeps into the sands of the Kalahari or travels down the Boteti River towards the Makgadikgadi Pans before it is also swallowed up by the desert. Most of the Delta's water comes from the distant Angolan highlands and moves so slowly that it does not follow the seasons: water levels are high in the dry season while during the rains, the levels are low. The Delta's gently flowing waters cross a sandy bed that filters the water, making it relatively clear and pure.

West of Botswana, the neighbouring country of Namibia embraces Southern Africa's second major desert. While the Kalahari is mostly flat, the Namib Desert boasts some spectacular dunescapes. At Sossusvlei, 100-storey-high dunes tower over the surrounding landscape. Shapes and shadows change forms, and colours change hues – from chocolate brown to burnt orange – as the sun burns off early morning fog. Although rainfall is almost non-existent, the regular fog and mist sustain animal, plant and insect life, many species of which have adapted specially to these unique conditions: using a headstand position atop sand dunes, the *toktokkie*, or tenebrionid beetle collects morning fog on its body and drinks when it reaches the lowest point – its head.

At the southern end of the desert lies the Fish River Canyon. To get to its main viewpoint, a gravel road leads up a long, gradual rise until abruptly, a massive void appears, like a colossal wound in the earth's crust. The base of the canyon is over half a kilometre (⅓ mile) below, and its far side up to 27 kilometres (17 miles) away. Further down the canyon lies Ai-Ais ('hot hot') springs, a popular resort that is closed over the summer months due to extreme temperatures and the risk of flash floods.

OPPOSITE *A dugout canoe, or* makoro, *is a tranquil way to explore the waterways and channels in Botswana's Okavango Delta.*

To the west of the Fish River Canyon a long, straight road crosses the uninhabited desert through the 'Sperrgebiet' (the forbidden diamond area) to the Atlantic coast. In searing temperatures, burning winds blow sand-drifts across the road from low dunes.

Ten kilometres (6 miles) from the coast, the road starts descending towards sea level and the temperature plummets. Instead of a green coastline, the desert meets the sea in a barren, rocky seashore. The cold, desolate coast seems a world away from the sweltering desert, just a few kilometres distant. Here, where the road ends, lies the isolated coastal town of Lüderitz, a German-styled fishing port. Despite the bleak coastline, the marine environment is rich with seals, dolphins and penguins, as well as plentiful catches of fish.

Inland from the coast, in the 'Sperrgebiet', are several desert 'ghost towns', including Kolmanskop. It was once a thriving diamond town where the local pub took payment in diamonds if a patron's money ran out. All manner of luxuries were brought in to Kolmanskop – from theatre groups all the way from Europe, to fresh water. But mining moved to Oranjemund and Kolmanskop's heydays are now long gone. Sand dunes push through its once plush mansions and winds whistle through empty hospital corridors.

A similarly eerie atmosphere pervades Namibia's Skeleton Coast. So called because of its skeletons of whales, ships and people, the often fog-bound coast has claimed dozens of ships over the years, with many mariners making it safely to land only to succumb to the barren, waterless desert that pushes right to the shoreline. At Cape Cross on the Skeleton Coast an impressive 100 000 Cape fur seals have made their home, thriving on the fish-rich waters that also attract recreational

LEFT *Massive dunes form a permanent barrier to the Tsauchab riverbed at Sossusvlei in Namibia's Namib Desert.*
ABOVE *Sand slowly covers Kolmanskop, an abandoned mining town in the Namib Desert.*

fishermen from far and wide. A 500-kilometre-long (300 miles) stretch of the Skeleton Coast has been declared the Skeleton Coast Park.

But it is the inland Etosha National Park that is Namibia's premier wildlife park. The massive 2.2-million-hectare (5.4 million acre) park is centred around Etosha ('Great White Place') Pan, an enormous salt pan which itself covers more than 6 000 square kilometres (2 300 square miles). To put these vast statistics

ABOVE *Once part of the ocean floor, South Africa's renowned Table Mountain overlooks Cape Town and the Cape Peninsula.*

into perspective, the park's boundary is 800 kilometres (500 miles) long. With several permanent waterholes, the park supports large numbers of wildlife despite its general dryness, and is a stronghold for the endangered cheetah and black rhino. Spotting game is easy in its

wide open spaces, but some of the best game-viewing can be enjoyed while waiting at a waterhole for the animals to come and drink.

Also in the north of Namibia is Kaokoland where the Himba people live – one of the most traditional groups of people on the continent. Using butterfat and ochre on their skin and hair, and dressed only in animal skins, the Himba are ethnically part of the larger Herero group who took on the beliefs and dress of the 19th-century German

missionaries. Herero women wear large, rolled cloth hats and voluminous full-length dresses. The contrast with their sub-group, the Himba, could not be more stark.

To the south of Namibia lies South Africa, a 'Rainbow Nation' made up of many different groups. The country boasts some of the most beautiful stretches of coastline on the continent, as well as offering a variety of landscapes ranging from desert to dramatic mountainous regions.

One of South Africa's best known and most impressive landmarks is Cape Town's Table Mountain. A 'tablecloth' of cloud often shrouds the flat-topped 1 073-metre-high (3 520 feet) mountain and a cable car ride to its summit provides spectacular views over the city, one of the most superbly sited in the world. As well as its beauty, Cape Town is also known for its superb beaches, historical architecture and mix of people. Southern Africa's first European settlement started in

Cape Town in 1652 and ever since then the strategically positioned city has had a bustling port. Today warehouses and wharves on the vibrant Waterfront have been developed into a lively area of bars, restaurants and shops. The tip of the Cape Peninsula embraces the popular Cape of Good Hope Nature Reserve.

Just inland from Cape Town is the attractive town of Stellenbosch which exudes charm and character with its traditional Cape Dutch buildings and shady, oak-lined streets. The

university town was first settled in the 1680s and since then Stellenbosch and the surrounding countryside have become synonymous with wine. The region boasts dozens of winelands, many with beautiful, old buildings and a spectacular backdrop of rugged mountains.

West of Stellenbosch along South Africa's West Coast lies Namaqualand, a region which stretches over both the Western and Northern Cape provinces. In August and September the

VISIONS OF AFRICA

usually arid landscape presents one of the most magnificent natural floral displays in the world. The drab land becomes carpeted in a dazzling show of spring wild flowers, as millions of orange, yellow, purple and pink flowers open up and follow the arc of the sun.

Also in the Northern Cape is the Kalahari Gemsbok National Park, created to protect the graceful gemsbok, or oryx. Bordering Namibia to the west, the park is contiguous with Botswana's Gemsbok National Park on its eastern side. Together the two parks form a massive protected area of the southern Kalahari Desert. Surprisingly, this dry and barren, although not completely vegetationless, park holds a considerable amount of game including all the major predators and a considerable antelope population.

Contrasting with the harsh, dry Kalahari is one of the greenest and most picturesque regions in South Africa – the Garden Route. Squeezed between the Indian Ocean and the Outeniqua and Tsitsikamma mountains, the area has a relatively wet, mild 'Mediterranean' climate – quite different from most of the African continent. Indigenous forests abound between the beaches and mountains, interspersed with rivers and lagoons.

Many nature reserves and parks have been set up along the Garden Route to preserve the forests and coastal scenery. The hundreds of walking tracks and hiking trails through these reserves are popular with walkers and bird-watchers, who can find a large variety of both forest and coastal species. It is also a favourite area for watersports.

RIGHT *South Africa's vast Kruger National Park boasts more wildlife species than any other park in Africa, including abundant giraffe and enormous herds of impala.*

146

Just east of the Garden Route is Jeffrey's Bay, known to surfers around the world for its superb rolling waves. Further up the coast and also popular with surfers is the city of Durban. A row of modern high-rise hotels line Durban's beaches in a 6-kilometre-stretch (4 miles) called the Golden Mile. The city's large Indian population imparts an Asian flavour to Durban, giving it an exotic touch with colourful bazaars and mosques.

Inland from Durban lies the dramatic Drakensberg, forming the most spectacular part of the Great Escarpment that marks the edge of the highveld. The 1 000-kilometre-long (620 miles) Drakensberg, once an ancient plateau, has eroded and weathered into breathtaking sheer cliffs, columns, pinnacles and peaks. The Zulu name of *uKhalamba* ('Barrier of Spears') is a good description of the mountains, although the Afrikaans word of *Drakensberg* ('Dragon Mountain') is no less evocative. With names like Giant's Castle, Cathedral Peak and Champagne Castle, the 'otherworldly' aspect of the Drakensberg is said to have given a very young J. R. R. Tolkien inspiration for his book *Lord of the Rings*.

The many reserves, parks and wilderness areas in the 'Berg', as it is called locally, are popular with hikers, and are known for their 'champagne air'. At high altitude the cool, fresh mountain air can become very cold indeed – frosts and snow are common.

Another major tourist attraction in South Africa is the Kruger National Park – with more than 2 000 kilometres (1 200 miles) of roads

and a total area of 19 485 square kilometres (7 523 square miles), the Kruger is one of the world's best known wildlife reserves.

Running over 300 kilometres (190 miles) north to south along the Mozambique border, the Kruger was originally set up a century ago thanks to the foresight of the then South African president Paul Kruger. The park not only has an enormous variety of fauna – more species than any other park in Africa – but it also has large numbers of many of those species. A night in one of Kruger's many camps is a quintessential African experience, the sound of lions roaring a memory that time will never erase.

Just 20 kilometres (12 miles) south of the Kruger lies Swaziland, bordered by South Africa on all sides, except for the east, which is bounded by Mozambique. It is one of Africa's few surviving monarchies. For such a tiny country, it has a significant variety of landscapes from hot, grassed lowlands to cool, forested mountains. Several reserves are well stocked with game, some with the added bonus of walking and horseback safaris.

Lesotho, to Swaziland's south, is completely surrounded by South Africa. Known as the 'Kingdom of the Sky', it boasts the highest mountain in Southern Africa, the 3 841-metre-high (12 600 feet) Mount Thabana-Ntlenyana. Lesotho is the source of the Orange River, but despite being relatively close to, and high above, the Indian Ocean, the river follows a much longer path. After flowing across nearly half of South Africa, it eventually forms the Namibian/South African border before finally discharging into the Atlantic Ocean, over 2 000 kilometres (1 200 miles) from its source.

As well as boasting some of the continent's best wildlife parks, Southern Africa is a rich and varied region, with magnificent flora, landscapes and wildlife, and a diverse and fascinating cultural heritage.

LEFT *Crisp mountain air and a landscape of spectacular proportions make hiking and climbing popular among the pinnacles and sheer cliffs of KwaZulu-Natal's Drakensberg.*

PREVIOUS PAGES   *Sunset over Lake Kariba's drowned forest. When the Zambezi River was dammed in the 1950s, the extra mass on the earth's crust caused minor earthquakes.*
LEFT   *Lechwe bound across shallow water in Botswana's Okavango Delta, a unique wetland in an arid land.*
ABOVE   *A lioness in the Gemsbok National Park, Botswana. Lions seldom move except to either hunt or drink.*
FOLLOWING PAGES   *Vast salt pans in Botswana are all that are left of what was once Africa's largest lake, although they do occasionally flood after heavy seasonal rains.*

LEFT *A Himba man surveys the vast, empty expanse of Kaokoland in Namibia, one of the country's most sparsely populated regions.*

ABOVE *Despite flowing for just one or two months a year, the Fish River has carved one of the world's most spectacular canyons, the Fish River Canyon in Namibia.*

FOLLOWING PAGES *Elephants in Namibia's Etosha National Park are some of the largest in Africa. Scientists believe that their longer legs are an adaptation for travelling long distances between water sources.*

PREVIOUS PAGES *Nature's Valley beach forms part of South Africa's lush Garden Route – a region known for its pristine beaches and coastline, indigenous forests, and abundant bird and marine life.*

OPPOSITE A *Zulu sangoma, or witchdoctor, in KwaZulu-Natal, South Africa. While some traditional medicines have no scientific base, they often have psychological benefits for patients.*

ABOVE *Married Ndebele women still wear brass and copper rings around their necks.*

FOLLOWING PAGES *Set in a beautiful and fertile valley below the Hex River Mountains in South Africa's Western Cape are some of the country's most productive vineyards.*

Ghana AFRICA

The designer coffins made by the Ga carpenters of southern Ghana are unique. The origin of these elaborate coffins stems from the sudden death of a chief and a grandmother's dream to fly in an aeroplane. In the 1950s, famous carpenter, Ata Owoo, was commissioned to make a cocoa pod palanquin for a chief, but the chief died before it was finished. It was thought only appropriate that he should ride in it for his last journey in this world. Inspired by this, when the grandmother of carpenter Seth Kane Kwei died, he had the idea of fulfilling her lifetime dream — to ride in an aeroplane. A nascent business emerged and coffins became a symbol of a person's work and status. Photographer SARAH ERRINGTON takes a look at the creations that honour and glorify the dead

Burial

Above: in Ga religion there are a number of different gods. The Woyo, or traditional priestess, Adjeley Coaltar who is buried in a mermaid coffin, looked after a shrine dedicated to the sea god Kanjar. The Woyo is the intermediary between also known as 'Long Journey' made the mermaid which has piercing blue eyes, long straight henna-ed hair, silver scales and little fish swimming up her stomach. Okai has a workshop in the backstreets of the fishing village of Teshie where he shares a

Above: the mother of Peter Borkety Kuwono, who died in a road accident, is comforted by one of her grandchildren. In Ghana, family support and public grieving is expected and normal. A funeral, often called a 'black wedding' is a great social event, a place to show off the latest fashions in hairstyle and clothes, and also a place for networking and perhaps to meet a future partner. The extravagant display is equally important for the living, to ensure that the wrath of the deceased will not be incurred. Death is not the end of life, but the beginning of another role, which may influence events among the family of the departed far more than their relative was ever able to do while still in

sights

Above: the funeral of Madam Susanna Dedei Lamptey, a lady cocoa farmer who was buried in a cocoa pod coffin. She is seen here lying in state and being given a message by a relative. As usual no expense has been spared to have a lavish funeral. There is even a music box playing beneath the bed. But to quote Paa Joe who made the tanker coffin for Peter Borkety Kuwono. "The importance of funerals is to celebrate a person's work in this life; a funeral must befit your stature. The shrouds, bed, coffin and drumming raises you on a pedestal. Whether rich or poor, the sort of position held determines the burial you deserve to bring honour and esteem to your family"

Peter Borkety Kuwono, or Blow, is buried in an exact wooden replica of the oil tanker in which he crashed in mysterious circumstances. A sudden death is rarely seen to be entirely of god's calling. A cousin who is a Wulomo, or a traditional priest, is left to find out the 'real' cause of death. These days certain consultations are done by mobile 'phone

Right: the wake of Adjeley Coaltar, the traditional priestess. As she lies in state she is surrounded by priestesses dressed in customary white, and novices in white headdresses who hold candles while chanting. A visit to a Woyo at her shrine is usually made to seek advice with family or personal problems or to redeem a curse. The Woyo will converse with her god and spirits on behalf of the living. Payment for a ceremony to call upon the god may be a bottle of schnapps, chickens, or sometimes a goat

In the workshop of the Kane Kwei brothers the finishing touches are put to an aeroplane coffin for an airline official. It was here that it all began. This is the home of the late Seth Kane Kwei, the most famous coffin maker of them all. He passed on his skills to his apprentices, his nephew Paa Joe, and to his three sons, two of whom now run the family business

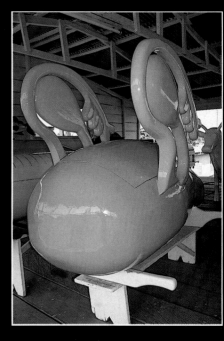

A chicken or hen coffin sits in Paa Joe's workshop. Unlike the mermaid which was a special order, the hen is a popular design usually kept in stock for a notable woman. The chicks represent the children. The matriarch of a family and mother of several children is highly respected. It is essential to have a funeral and a coffin deserving and representative of such status

Paa Willie stands beside his favourite coffin, the Mercedes Benz, with the number plate R.I.P. This is often the choice of the family of a businessman, regardless of whether or not he owned a Mercedes. Paa Willie's '6ft Enterprise' as he calls his business, is situated next to the hairdresssers, 'Mummy To Salon', and above the 'Home Sweet Chop Bar', owned by Paa Joe's wife Elizabeth

A womb coffin awaits its rightful occupant at Paa Joe's workshop. "It was a woman's doctor [a gynaecologist] from overseas who asked me to make this for her," says Paa Joe. "She will put it on display until she needs it for herself. I didn't know what a womb looked like so I asked the doctor to send me a photo which I then copied." Coffins are made by memorising a design or by copying a photo. The shapes are drawn freehand on pieces of wood which are then cut and glued together before being sanded and painted. Immense trouble is taken to get every detail accurate. The workshops of the coffin makers have become a tourist attraction and receive famous visitors. Paa Joe has already had a visit from ex-US president Jimmy Carter